Dare to Be a Millionaire

How Doing What You Love Can Make You Rich!

The Twenty Year Plan

By

Dr. Robert L. Lawson

Dare to Be a Millionaire

Printed and Distributed by
The Educational Publisher Inc.
Columbus, Ohio
www.EduPublisher.com

ISBN: 1-934849-30-8
ISBN13: 978-1-934849-30-9

Table of Contents

Dare to Be a Millionaire

Acknowledgments

Firstly, I wish to acknowledge God through his son Jesus Christ as my almighty creator. It is God who gives me breath and allows me to live and utilize my talents, gifts, skills and abilities to benefit others. I am so deeply grateful and thankful for that.

I want to acknowledge my wife, Shannon, without whose love and support I would not be successful. Most successful people have a supportive spouse. I love my wife and my three sons, Robert Jr., James and Michael, and a very special friend, Dr. Dan Evans.

I want to acknowledge my mother, Mary Irene Payne, My aunt Nora Faye Lawson, My uncle, Hollis Lawson and my grandmother, Ethel Wilson Lawson who have all inspired me greatly. I love them dearly. To all of my professional colleagues at the Zip Publishing Company, without your professional assistance in terms of format, design and marketing, this manuscript would never have made it to market. Because of you, people all over the world can read this book.

People often ask me where my inspiration comes from. In addition to my family, I receive tremendous inspiration and amazing ideas from my students from around the world. It is because of my students and my professional peers that I am as successful as I am.

The environments in which I currently work at Georgetown Jr-Sr. High School in Georgetown, Ohio and Ohio University in Chillicothe, Ohio and

Zanesville, Ohio provide three of the absolute best educational opportunities imaginable.

My professional friends, Perianne Germann, Jerry Underwood, Diane Lewis, Holly Woodruff, Chad McKibben, Melissa Cropper, Andrea Faulkner, Jessica McNair, Susan Noll, Matt Cameron, Joyce Smith, Kelly Tomlin, Shawn Tomlin, Tanya Haughaboo, Brady Womack, Aaron Kitchen, Mark and Tracee Garrett, Aleta Mays Polley, Harvey Alston, Ella Coleman, Tom Ramey, Jim Tillman, Brenda Dixon, Mike Fadeley, Gar Seigla, Carrie Hudson, Karen Colwell, Debbie Gardner, Bea Wheatley, Kathleen Cahall, Robin Bohl, Brent Caldwell, Matt Carpenter, Deanna Schrag, Jennifer Shively, Robert Thomas, Lee Walters, Howard Willis, Kathy Zurbuch, Joyce Beacraft, Dorella Grant, Tony Dunn, Rebecca Honaker, John Copas, Andy Creighton, Donna Devries, Tony Henson, Stephen Hahn, Donna Hawkins, Coach Hawkins, Christy Lucas, Queda Knuckles, Jamie Louden, Sherry Nawrocki, Sandra Reedy, Bonnie Davis, Robin Swartz, Lynn Decker, Cary Gray, Heather Bertram, Mike Jennings, Dr. Dale Nietzschke Beth Lahmer, Candy Decker, Cathy Chadwell, Bernie Cropper, Wanda and Wilson Mollfulleda, Kim Conner, Karen Collins, Betsy Gosnell, Lori Keller, Cindy Oliver, Janet Fink, Karen Virgin, Kim McKimmey, Richard Holt, Peggy Rowe, Kim Riley, Lucius Lewis, Dennis Fravel, Roger Ford, Dr. Leonard Deutsch, Dr. Sarah Denman, Dr. Carolyn Hunter, Dr. Betty Jo Jarrell, Nedra Lowe, Peggy Wilmink, Russ Gaskins, Kim Henry, Gene Murphy, Tony Murphy, Robin Murphy, Marvin O. Mitchell, Joan Adkins, Dr. F. David Wilkin, Marvin Moore, Elaine Armstrong, Gene Armstrong, Wendell Payne, Keith Payne, Gene Payne, Rita Payne, Dr. Greg Sojka, Dr. Barry Dorsey, Dr. Clyde Evans, Sarah Evans, Nancy Evans, Rosemary Evans, Judge

Margaret Evans, Susan Epling, Eric Toole, Rachel Higgins, Joyce Weichelman, Tammy Davis, Mark Cornell, Allen Rutz, Eugene Rutz, Kent Shawver, Keith McGuire, Brent Saunders, Arius Hurt, Dianna Holmes, Martha Frampton, Reverend Hill, Frank Beach, Opal Lloyd, Lloyd Myers, Paige Sheets, Lois Sheets, Keith Carter, Jerry Rusk, Ed Sayre, Jack Finch, Connie Bradbury, Chuck Bradbury, Doug Kuhn, Jodi Vanwinkle, Gene Beckett, Steve McCain, Sherry McCain, Dr. Velta Kelly, Arley Owens, Ralph Kraus, Audris Billberry, Mike Vance, Sandra Kellam, Willie Kellam, Doug Poage, Jim Garrett, Tina Hoskey, Sue Eubanks, Jessie Payne, Eleanor Keels, Clinton Hearns, Margaret Hearns, Rev. Parker, Pat Parker, Mother Woods, Carmen Josey, Deacon Josey, Hazel Richardson, Sue Hegarty, Marcia Harris, Hector Flores, Candy McBride, Rev. Trotter, Sandra Trotter, Nedra Davis, Coy Bacon, Donna Coles, Elaine Jones, Susan Stasiak, Dee Hammel, Martha Cosby, Ilinda Reese, Henry Ford, Bill Heaberlin, Dr. A.L. Addington, Dr. Clive Veri, Elder Ralph Clay, Brenda Johnson, Lonnell Johnson, Al Oliver, Patricia Carson, Theresa Fennell, Gonelcha Askew, Cindi Holodnak,, Don Starr, Kathy Cain, Holly Thompson, Ernie Adams, Teresa Hilderbrand, Roy Taylor, Sue Ann Baird, Rita Haubell, Pat Spradlin, Darrell Brooks, Tracy Keene, Warren Armsted, Steven Geib, Dru Whittaker, Teresa Lewis, Janice Mercier, Joyce Atwood, Paul Lloyd, Nedra Davis, Peggy Rowe, the Strom Family, Cory Frederick, Paul Lloyd, Larry Artrip, Dr. Peter Mills, Dr. Dagmar Pelzer, Bob Willey, Patsy Schultz, Jane Ann Slagle, Mark Graham, John Cooper, Judy Reich, Don Reich, the Mealy Family, Susan Haft, Beverly Crabtree, Jack Payton, Jim Osborne, Tom Walker, Bill Wamsley, Lori Meadows, Bridget Hennessey, Lori Naskey, Norm Persin, Kristin Depenbrock, Mark Clifford, Curt Clifford, Meghan

Poling, Rondea Miller, Ann-Marie Shaffer, Sharee Price, Chuck Burke, Tina Frease, Ralph Sininger, Steven Dunkin, Dick Colwell, Dr. Jeffrey S. Donohoo, Dr. Raymond Virost, Michael H. Smith, Patricia Hardyman, Sherry Marks, Terry Graham, Rebecca L. Honaker, Debbe Gardner, Rachel Underwood, Steve Roese and Larry Artrip and many, many, many other individuals who are just simply too numerous to mention here.

A very special thanks to Dean BeBee, Mike Lafreniere and Jack Jeffery for insuring that this book project and seminar was exposed to a much, much larger viewing audience than I would have ever anticipated, especially Mike Lafreniere whose interests in my works have been unwavering since the day we first met. Thank you, thank you, thank you and now, let's go and enjoy this awesome journey together. One of life's most important lessons is to never forget the people who assisted you on your journey.

Introduction

When I began my teaching career in 1973, there were two expressions that I lived by which have since become staunch stalwarts as a part of the philosophy I use to navigate life. Now, I am applying them to my finances as well. One aphorism or wise expression that I use is "Preparation is the key to success." The other is Dr. Robert Schuller's possibility thinker's creed which is as follows: "When faced with a mountain, I will not quit. I will keep on striving until I climb over, find a pass through, tunnel underneath or stay and turn the mountain into a goldmine with God's help."

Both of these amazingly insightful quotes coupled with one of Anthony Robbins' favorite expressions, "Repetition is the mother of skill," have served me well over the years. Allow me to use the analogy of building a muscle and building wealth to illustrate the correlation between the two. If one develops an exercise program and lifts a certain amount of weight over and over and over, that muscle will eventually grow in response. If one is preparing to teach a class, one spends time reading and reviewing materials that pertain specifically to that class. Whether it is a mental, a physical activity or a combination of both, the activities are designed to achieve the same result.

The more a particular thing is repeated over and over and over, the more it becomes a functional autonomy (habit). Henry David Thoreau, the prolific writer said it this way. "As a single footstep will not make a path on the earth, so a single thought will not make a pathway in the mind. To make a deep physical path, we must walk again and again. To make a deep mental path, we must think over and over again the kinds of thoughts we wish to dominate our lives."

The same process is required if one expects to acquire an abundance of wealth. Individuals go throughout life on a daily basis and they read, they earn, they save, they invest and they retire. If they have made most of the right moves, they can spend their lives doing what they enjoy most because they have figured out the most effective ways to make their money work for them. That is exactly what this book is all about.

This exciting and informative book will show you a step-by-step process on effective ways to build wealth. As you read through this book, you will encounter constant reminders on what you need to do to stay focused and on task in order to realize your financial goals sooner. Sometimes, you have to follow the advice you give to others just to make sure that it works. This product that you are currently holding in your hands is proof enough for me that the processes I share with you do actually work. If they did not, I would never have finished this book!

Con artists are a dime a dozen in today's society and I'm placing bets that when you finish the content in this book, one of the things you will discover is that it's the real deal. This is one particular way in which a person can achieve some or all of his or her lifetime objectives. Unfortunately, as most people would like for you to believe, there are no get rich quick schemes. There's just a simple steady process that has worked for the wealthy since the beginning of time. Why should all of us not know about the same selective principles? We should.

Through the research that I have conducted and the statistics that I will reveal through years of arduous compilation, thorough study and review, this book will inform your real life experience with information that is critical to the establishment of a wealth oriented consciousness. You can start today and employ a number of strategies that will enable you to earn, save and invest your dollars wisely.

When you pay money for a course in which you enroll, don't you expect to get something beneficial out of it? The obvious answer is yes or you would never have enrolled in the first place. The same principle is true for this book which you have bought. What you get should be of even greater benefit than what you've paid. In other words, you should yield a higher return on the investment you've made in yourself. Even if you just read something that reinforces the common sense ideas that you already know, you might be inspired to take action just because of what you've read. If you do, that puts you ahead of the game.

Will I make money on this book that you purchase? Yes, I will, but, I'm not trying to hide that fact. If you can sense when materials are of significant value, you should purchase them. Not only should you purchase them but if you are really sold on the message and the overall content, you should get more to spread the word because you've stumbled onto something that is really, really, effective.

Unlike many other products, this book provides you with a specific goal achievement strategy for the acquisition of money not just through real estate or the insurance industry but specifically how to pursue other areas of interest that may be more significant to you. Following your own dream to achieve financial independence can make all the difference in the world. In essence, this book constitutes a very practical "how to" guide that further augments your current knowledge base by sharing with you case studies that are highly relevant to the acquisition of wealth.

In preparing these materials for you, I have made every effort to probe some of the best minds in the world to discover some of their amazing ideas on wealth accumulation. Here's just a small sampling of a few of the materials I've perused in preparing and you may very well recognize some of the titles, authors or personalities which include but are not limited to Venita Van Caspel's New Money Dynamics, Think and Grow Rich by Napoleon Hill, Rich Dad, Poor Dad, The Millionaire Mind, The Millionaire Next Door, the Susie Ormond Television Show or her book on Nine Strategies for Building Wealth, Charles Givens' book entitled Wealth Without Risk or another one he wrote entitled More Wealth Without Risk, Sylvia Porter's Money Book, Peter McWilliams's Wealth 101 and watching and reading about Oprah Winfrey, Warren Buffet, Bill and Linda Gates and Donald Trump. These are literally some of the best known personalities in our society and what they discuss and talk about works! That's why I have listed them here.

Not only that, but there are millions and millions of successful people in our society and most of them we have never heard of nor will we. You may very well be one of those people. The energy that has enabled me to create these materials comes as a direct result of the confidence I have gained by watching these principles work in my own life. I don't know how else to say it. These time-honored principles really do work. Once you have actually discovered this for yourself, what an incredible gift you will have to share with others on any given day of the year. Whether it's Christmas, Father's Day, Mother's Day, someone's birthday or other, you can give the gift, Dare to Be a Millionaire. What a great thing you will be able to do to help others improve their financial situation through learned discipline. It will give new meaning to the phrase, "Discipline is Freedom." Here's the challenge. Not many want to dare to be a millionaire and have you ever stopped to ask the question, Why Not? Maybe that's the problem. It was the great E.E. Channing who once said, "Sometimes, to dare is the highest wisdom." Well, I dare, do you? Embrace the idea. You could do it!

Good luck on your new financial journey and in your quest to sow seeds of harmony, good will and prosperity into the lives of others. The old Danish proverb is loaded with meaning. "Give a man a fish and he will eat for a day but if you teach him how to fish, he can eat for a lifetime."

The Challenges We Face

"Patience is the key element of success."

Bill Gates

Throughout the years, many in our society have been duped because they have bought into one get rich quick scheme after another. The truth of the matter is quite simple. In spite of what you might hear or a sweet deal that sounds like it's too good to be true, there are no fool proof get rich quick schemes. Most folks have been badly burned at one time or another because of the microwave mentality that has captivated the masses. We want what we want and we want it right now. That's the problem. As a general rule, nothing really great happens over night. It takes years and years and years of strict discipline and adherence to a process that is virtually foolproof. There are no shortcuts to achieving financial freedom.

Americans and populations of other great countries around the world are bombarded daily by the multi- mass media magnates whom we listen to on the radios, watch on our TV's and invite into our bedrooms on the internet. All try daily or nightly to tempt us with their quick-fix solutions to today's challenges because they are highly aware of our instant gratification fix. And all the while, our country suffers from high rates of unemployment and our housing industry may improve but, right now, it is in shambles. That's the downside.

The side you're not hearing much about though is the upside. Even during these deep, dark and somewhat disheartening times, fortunes are still being made. It happened during the crash of the 1929 stock market and it's happening right now as you read this book. People are making money and they are making a ton of it.

The news commentators who frequent our T.V. screens and other modes of communication are well dressed, well groomed, well coached and well fed. And there's a good reason this is so. They have earned the right to be there and they are prospering well. Here's the good news. You should be prospering well too. Even in the midst of tough economic times, you can do well.

As millions of homes continue to be foreclosed upon and as the unemployment rate continues to escalate, small businesses, the very heart and essence of the American Dream and enterprise system is all but on life support. The growth of our business enterprises has stagnated because current market conditions will not support the hiring of new employees, lending institutions don't have the desire to assume greater risks beyond what they have already incurred and to further exacerbate the current dilemma we face, thousands of individuals have either lost their jobs or are in danger of losing them because of inadequate funding and diminishing state revenue. A picture of pure devastation has been painted for us to observe and if we buy into it, we are doomed.

Here's the really good news. We do not have to buy into it. When we scrutinize closely the flip side of this two-headed coin, we will see that in spite of this seemingly abysmal portrayal of our current economy, there are still many whose creative and innovative tendencies enable them to prosper.

It's true that much of that optimism is housed on wall street but numerous opportunities are in abundance on main street as well and this book will show you exactly what you must do to take full advantage of those opportunities.

Some insurance companies and some health care industries, for example, according to which report you read are reporting a 56% profit in revenues that are generated in excess of expenditures while the CEO's of some elite companies receive bonuses in the millions of dollars. Even the automotive industry after facing reeling declines is on the rebound. This resilience is a staple of how we do business in spite of tough situations. It is as Dr. Robert Schuller has said, "Tough times never last but tough people do." Those of us who have plans to achieve high level success in life need those kinds of encouraging words from time to time to keep us going in the face of adversity.

In a competitive market driven economy such as ours, even in tough economic times, the law of supply and demand is still very much at work. There has never been nor will there ever be an equal distribution of wealth. There are certain professional athletes, coaches and entertainers who earn millions of dollars annually. These salaries are determined by a number of factors which are performance based, incentive laden and driven by high expectations, customer satisfaction and the potential for high revenue production. It is an intensely high risk, high reward arena and when the reward does not exceed the risk factors, both the entertainment industry and the athletic industry act swiftly to right the ship. It is an incredibly tough and volatile environment and decisions are made daily based on results or the lack thereof. The intent is always to find creative ways to generate more revenue and many times it comes at the expense of paying customers.

Instead of remaining a captive in a poor economy, it is time for as many as possible to take more initiative and more advantage of the opportunities that are now available. If you have been laid off from work or you are still amongst the ranks of the chronically unemployed or underemployed, the bottom line is this.

As I said in my first book, *Destined for Greatness*, "Belief is the one foundational key to all of success. Given that fact, you still have to believe that you can turn the tide and make something good happen for you and your family because you can and this book will explain precisely how you can do that.

We must look for opportunities when they come and when they don't come, we must make them. It was Shakespeare who said in his play, "Julius Caesar" "There is a tide in the affairs of men which taken at the flood leads on to fortune; Omitted, all the voyage of their life is bound in shallows and in miseries. On such a full sea are we now afloat. And we must take the current when it serves or lose our ventures."

At this precise moment in our history, truer words were never spoken. It is we who must rise up and take full responsibility for what happens in our own lives. We must rise up and meet the current challenge we face with full vengeance. We must take the initiative to step out, to be bold, to take risks and not die with our music still left in our souls. We must not die with our best songs still left unsung and still housed in the confines of our hearts. No, that would be the great tragedy and the great travesty of epic proportions. No, others should hear our music before we are finished in this life.

It must not be business as usual. You must become more resourceful, more inventive, more creative and more perceptive in your daily ventures. Just recently, I finished reading Dr. Wayne Dyer's latest book entitled, *Excuses Begone.* It is a powerful book that provides those who read it with the tools necessary to make an important paradigm shift in the way they approach life's challenges.

One of Dr. Dyer's chapters ends with the following quote. "When you change the way you look at things, the things you look at change." That one statement alone could be the catalyst that places you back on the road to success if it causes you to shift the attitude of your thinking in an effort to dig your way out of a rut in which you find yourself.

Regarding the science of human behavior and the psychology of human achievement, I have encountered numerous individuals who have reached the depths of despondency and were ready to quit, give up, throw in the towel so to speak because life had chased them into a corner and reduced them to a state of helplessness only to be rejuvenated again by a sudden burst of inspiration obtained from a quote, a specific strategy for action or other noteworthy event that somehow helped them to realize that there are still opportunities for them to pursue, that all is not lost.

One of the very best ways for individuals to further enhance their opportunities for success is by returning to the classroom and discovering that they are not alone in this huge world of hurt and disillusionment and that yes, there are still a plethora of opportunities that abound in other fields. They just have to get involved and understand that a job loss or other significant catastrophic event that has occurred is still not the end of the world. There is still hope. In spite of the fact that there are millions of books in today's marketplace, that is precisely why I wrote this one. The American psychologist William James penned these magnificent words. "The greatest discovery of our generation is that we can alter our lives by altering our attitudes of mind." Let's get started right now!

Getting Started

> "To get what we've never had, we must do what we've never done."

One of the most important chapters in this book is the one you are reading right now. I say that at age 60 with a great deal of seriousness. I have gotten started with saving and investing dollars, have you?

Although, I am doing well, had I started in my 20's or my 30's, I would have accumulated an even greater abundance of financial wealth. Many of us continue to make the same excuses as to why we do not save our money, year after year after year.

We simply never develop the discipline and the commitment that are necessary and essential to address our financial and economic needs. For some nebulous reason, we never seem to grasp the importance of the freedom and flexibility managing our money effectively affords us in later years.

Early in life, most of us don't have that kind of vision nor do we possess a desire that is strong enough that makes us want to save more. Those of us who do, get to the point where we understand the significance and power of having an abundance of economic wealth and soon realize what an amazing advantage it provides over the course of a lifetime.

With an abundance of money as your servant, you can accomplish a myriad of great things not only for yourself but for all of those who reside within your sphere of influence. Your money will also have an opportunity to grow in direct proportion to your level of benevolence and your mastery of the principles discussed in this book.

Having additional revenue provides you with life options that are inconceivable to those who live from paycheck to paycheck wondering how they will continue to pay their mortgage before their home goes into foreclosure. With those who are in the category of the chronically unemployed and have been looking for jobs for years, conditions are quite frankly deplorable.

It is time then to do everything within your power to start taking control of your economic future and be in a position to provide for yourself, for those you love and for those individuals and those organizations you have a desire to help.

There are numerous definitions of success. In Paul Hersey and Ken Blanchard's masterpiece, *The Management of Organizational Behavior*, success is defined as the progressive realization of a worthy goal. That is truly an excellent statement. Those who would be successful are those who are always in the process of succeeding. In other words, when the truly successful people reach their mark, they set another goal. With them, it is a habit. There are probably as many definitions of success as there are people on the planet. Given that rationale then, success is nothing more than a state of mind. Ultimately, you are the one who has to make the decision about what's important to you, what your values are, what you hope to achieve in life and whether or not you intend to try and fool people by just doing enough to get by or understand as soon as possible that the folks in this world who are really successful capitalize fully on the opportunities that avail themselves to them to get a good education and then apply their skills to the point where they utterly destroy their competition because they understand what the pursuit of excellence means.

I recently read an insightful article on the internet. The idea that left an indelible impression upon my mind was this. You might have an individual who owns a business and generates over $3,000,000 in capital per year, turns a reasonable profit and somehow feels that he is just scraping by because his attitude pertaining to his standard of living is just not fulfilling, gratifying or satisfying. That's a shame. It's a shame because his perception of himself and his definition of success are at odds. Charles J. Stanley, in his highly informative book, *The Millionaire Mind*, refers to this individual as an (UAW) under accumulator of wealth. This individual is an incredibly poor manager of not only his thinking process but also his economic resources. Unfortunately, our world is full of individuals like this. The more they get, the more they want and they have absolutely no idea how to enjoy the riches they have accumulated. These folks will never realize an opportunity to be fully satisfied and appreciative for what they have because they have simply not mastered the concept of living below their means. Their frame of reference is limited.

Stanley, through his research, discusses another type of millionaire mentality. It is the kind of mentality that I hope you can aspire to have. It is the (PAW) or the prodigious accumulator of wealth. If you have the desire to be a millionaire, that's the kind of millionaire you want to be. A prodigious accumulator of wealth knows exactly how to live below his means; he knows precisely how to permit his money to work for him and he does not spend money frivolously nor does he develop the bad habits shared by under accumulators of wealth.

Note the difference in attitude. The internet article also profiled an individual who worked a regular job and earned less than $45,000.00 per year. It's a stark contrast to our case study of the millionaire; however, this individual felt quite good about his earning potential as well as a high degree of satisfaction that he received through his job as a result of helping other people. He loved what he was doing. This gives great credence to the notion or idea of success being nothing more than a state of mind. In other words, an individual can be just about as happy as he makes up his mind to be. The intangible quality of success is elusive and what one seeks to achieve can only be validated by an individual's internal perception of life and how he makes sense of, interprets and acquires meaning from his world. Perceptions vary and the meaning of success is inherently different for each individual. Years ago, I stumbled across another interesting definition of success that I enjoy sharing with others. I find it particularly poignant as well as pregnant with possibility. "Success is the capacity within to take what was once only imagined and make it real." The intent of this book is to get people to act.

The first and most important step in building wealth lies in proving to yourself that you have the power, the ability and the skill to not only earn money but the power to save as well. Demonstrating to myself that I had the ability not only to earn money but to save money was the catalyst that enabled me to change my perception and my whole attitude about money, how I was handling it and what I needed to do next. Actually, there was no one else that I needed to prove anything to other than myself.

What do you believe? It is my belief that in order to develop a passion for making positive changes in your life that you need to experience some situations that drive you to want to take more control over your finances. Has anything ever happened to you that has made you want to do that? If so, what was it? Or were there a number of things? If enough events happen, you will begin to make constructive changes.

A number of things have happened in my life that have helped me to realize that if I want something then I am going to have to be the one who takes the initiative to get things done. When I reflect on those situations now, I am no longer bitter about them. I have learned from them and now feel that I am a better person as a result. My character has improved along the way. Thus, I am wealthier in many ways. Let me share one of the life-changing catalysts for me.

Several years ago, some immediate members of my family received a financial allotment from a will. At least one of those allotments was in the $50,000.00 range. Although it doesn't seem like a large sum of money, it was certainly more than I had ever seen at one time. I was told by a close family member that I needn't worry, that a portion of that would be shared with me. I wasn't sure what that meant but I got more excited than I should have because my expectations were somewhat misguided. That was my fault. (I promise—it won't happen again). One Christmas, someone gave me $200.00 from that $50,000.00 allotment.

Obviously, looking back on it now, I should have been nothing but grateful and thankful but, I wasn't. I certainly had a lot of growing to do. I was angry and upset but, I had no right to be. It wasn't my money.

I learned an awesome lesson though. My spirit was suddenly fueled with determination and unspeakable energy. It was at that point in my life than I realized something that was incredibly and remarkably profound. If I ever wanted to have $50,000.00 of my own money as discretionary income to spend however I wanted, I was simply going to have to earn it myself. I am not quite sure why that particular thought had never occurred to me before. Imagine that!

Today, I tell you that I am indeed most grateful for that exceptionally revealing and powerful eye opener! After all, God had certainly endowed me with amazing talents, skills and abilities. Why was I not using them in the manner that I should? Perhaps you can ask yourself the same question? Why are you not stirring up your own internal gifts and exercising them to their maximum potential. All I can say is this. Once you begin to discover and utilize the great internal gifts which you have been given and have made the decision to bring them to the surface, great things are going to happen.

The good old philosopher, Thomas Aquinas knew exactly what he was talking about back in the 1200's when he made this bold statement. "Pray as if everything depends upon God and then work as if everything depends upon you." Though I want my heart to be the kind of heart that freely gives to others without expecting anything in return, I never again want to have the mindset where I expect someone to give me something for nothing.

I have discovered in life that there are two kinds of people; there are producers and there are consumers. Consumers will take and take and take; they will spend and spend and spend without any thought about tomorrow. What kind of person are you? Are you a producer or a consumer? There's a part of me that honestly feels that without having had the experience that I previously shared with you, this book may not have been written. Here's my question for you then. What can be the igniter that lights your fire when it comes to the way you handle and produce revenue?

This book is replete with powerful ideas that can help you not only to take control of your financial life but virtually any area of your life over which you desire to have control. Do I still give to others who never gave to me? The answer is yes. In fact, I think that one of the best ways to measure success and to maintain a good sense of humility is to find others whom you can assist who will never be in a position to do anything for you in return. This in essence embodies the spirit of true giving. I do not consider myself any better than anyone else; I just happen to think differently about certain things. How about you? Do you think enough of yourself to start building toward your own future right now by taking the necessary and essential steps you must take today? This book will show you exactly how.

I am not an investment specialist and I have no intention of ever becoming one. That is not my forte; however, I have surrounded myself with certain individuals who specialize in the financial industry and with companies that have an incredible track record. My money is in good hands. It is in the hands of companies like TIAA/CREF, NEW YORK LIFE and the HARTFORD via Fifth Third Bank.

When you've proven to yourself that you have the ability to save money, then you are ready to take the next step, investing. The desire will begin to grow in you because you are cultivating a new found interest and one that works toward the expedition of your freedom and liberation. This is when you will begin to search and find those companies that have a proven track record and can assist you with your financial endeavors.

Whereas their expertise lies in ways to assist you in obtaining a good return on your investment, my expertise lies in the true development of human potential. My job is to build you and help you to position yourself to grow your finances; their job will be to assist you by helping your finances to grow.

What Motivates You?

"Fortune favors the bold."

Virgil

People often ask me, "What is it that motivates you?" I have pondered long and often on that question throughout the years and although the answer is multifaceted, for me, I must admit to you that a lot of my drive, determination and fire is intrinsic. It comes from within. It was Emerson who said, "What lies behind us and what lies before us are tiny matters compared to what lies within us."

I have also discovered over the years and throughout my life that a large amount of that intrinsic motivation was ignited in response to external triggers. In essence, I have been able to identify certain catalysts in my life that continue to cause me to compete with myself in an attempt to make what it is that I do for others even better. People often ask, "Why are you so excited at this early hour of the morning?" You always seem to have a smile on your face. I want what you've got. Let me give you some insight into my life about how the electric neurons are firing inside of my head.

Firstly, I am deeply honored that God has chosen me to be a beacon of light that does its best to shine on and for others. I am thrilled to have the opportunity to make positive deposits in the lives of others that far outshines the negatives you get from others who will give them to you freely and without your even asking. I am further emboldened in my quest and empowered by the support and inspiration that I receive from God, my family, my colleagues with whom I work and from my amazing and incredible students from in the classrooms and all around the world in their various walks of life.

Here's a small taste of how that has worked over the years in my life. When my students succeed in life, it has a very profound impact upon me. It provides me with the impetus I need to continue my journey. The most interesting and intriguing thing about life is that all the voyages or journeys upon which we embark are inherently different; however, if there is something in this text that I am writing that you can learn from vicariously as a result of the experiences that I share and you can wind up making the principles applicable to your own life by taking something valuable away, then this book will have served one of its primary purposes.

In the early 1970's when I began my career as an educator at Gallia Academy High School in Gallipolis, Ohio, I had the fortunate pleasure of having a straight "A" student by the name of Alan Rutz in one of my 7th grade English classes. At the midpoint of the year, I asked my students to evaluate the class and share their ideas on what they thought would improve the class.

While most students spent a lot of time crafting a long response, Alan was finished momentarily which made me wonder what he could possibly have written in such a succinct period of time. I was anxious to see. When my students exited the room and I flipped Alan's paper over to see what he had said, these words were written. "It is hard to describe perfection." I was only 22 years of age at the time. I am sixty years old as of this writing. Obviously, I have never forgotten that. Those words carved an indelible impression upon my memory forever and have since informed and influenced my life experiences and have spurred me on to greater achievement.

Those words came from one of my most intellectually gifted students. Do you have even a remote idea of what that does to a young teacher's confidence level when he is just beginning his teaching career? It had a most powerful and lasting impact upon my mental psyche. To have garnered the respect and admiration of one of my most perspicacious students just made me want to do even more with my life. Alan truly made me feel that I was making a difference. How do the people with whom you have surrounded yourself make you feel?

In your quest to acquire wealth as you dare to be a millionaire, I share these stories with you so you can see how they keep the fire burning in my life. I am sure you have your own stories and they can keep your fire lit and burning brightly as well. Think about some of them occasionally as you continue to move forward.

Years later, decades in fact, after I had moved on from Gallia Academy High School, Marshall University, Shawnee State University and into building my own consulting firm, I would receive a post card from a student that would strongly influence my decision to return to the classroom on a fulltime basis. I received this letter in 2005.

"Dear Mr. Lawson,

I hope this note finds you well. It's late, I've already written several drafts of this letter and I'm frustrated to find the right words. After all, I am writing to an English teacher. Since I spent a fair amount of time researching your address, I know I should just plow through to the next paragraph rather than contemplate the meaning of the words contained in the shards of my shrinking eraser. I want to thank you.

Apparently when you turn forty you acquire a rearview mirror to have a look at the past. I found myself wandering through a jungle of memories about growing up in a small town in the middle of nowhere, a seemingly idyllic enough spot known as Gallipolis.

I was aimlessly scrambling through the undergrowth of different varieties of choice and influences when I came upon a question:
Who have been my teachers? Of course there are teachers of all sorts throughout one's life but I recognized a kernel of truth about myself that I attribute to you.

Almost 30 years ago you were my eighth grade English teacher in Gallipolis – an awful grade during such a difficult phase of trying to grow up. It's not that I can remember the particular curriculum you taught, or that I had more or less success in your class than in other years. It was your infectious enthusiasm to teach and to learn that got me, and has since influenced and informed so many subsequent decisions I've made.

I also remember that for the first time, here was an adult truly engaged in school and the process of learning. And maybe also for the first time, a teacher who challenged me—not just to finish my work to the class standard but to my own.

These two gifts, the thirst to learn and to set my own standards, are truly empowering. I left Gallipolis promptly after graduation 25 years ago and since then I've managed to graduate from the University of Chicago with a liberal arts degree, traveled extensively all over the world, and most recently, returned to school to get a master's degree in architecture.

I really don't think that I would have made the same choices, decisions I value highly, were it not for your passion, skill and professionalism as a teacher.

I have never gone back to that strange Brigadoon(as I've come to think of Gallipolis) but sometimes I admit I'm curious and maybe someday, I'll get back for a visit—maybe to take the traditional half-time wagon ride of old fogies during the big homecoming game---and definitely still get the occasional craving for a footlong from Remo's hotdogs sometime soon.

I've had many teachers – some are considered brilliant thinkers and others exude enthusiasm, but, all things considered, I think you have been the best. So, Mr. Lawson, thank you. I just wanted you to know of at least one of those students so eager to get out of class and on to anything else, took away something they hold dear and appreciates your good work. Thank you again.

Sincerely,

Mark Cornell

So, again I ask. What is it that motivates you, that drives you, that propels you forward? My students have played a most significant and pivotal role in my success. They believe in me and I believe in them. It is a mutually beneficial professional working relationship and it is extremely powerful.

Because of my students, I have mastered my craft to the point where I can actually observe attitudinal changes in someone's disposition in a one day seminar. Many students have shared with me both verbally and through their writing that they sometimes enroll in a one hour credit class just to obtain the credit. Sometimes, it's early on a Saturday morning and that's the last place they would prefer to be. They arrive with low or no expectations of what will transpire in the next seven or eight hours and yet, for those who have serious intent, they leave rejuvenated beyond belief and a renewed dedication to either find or achieve their ultimate purpose in life. Those are the moments for which I live.

My wife, Shannon, my top admirer as well as my chief critic (Someone has to keep my feet firmly planted on the ground so that I can remain centered and focused) finds it amazing to be skilled to the point where you can truly make a positive impact upon someone's life within an eight hour setting and yet it is possible for that to happen. It is one of the things that gives me inspiration and keeps me going. If I am going to be a catalyst for positive change in a person's life then let me make it happen that way.

Further evidence of how this works occurred in a recent course I was teaching at Ohio University's Zanesville branch in Zanesville, Ohio. I was teaching a course that I had created entitled **Maximizing Your Potential for Greatness.** Although, there are literally hundreds of student responses I could have chosen to share with you over the years, I felt that this one places everything in its proper perspective.

The point is this. We don't know how much time we have here. Our days are numbered and I figure that we ought to embrace the sense of urgency in doing constructive things while the opportunity still exists for that time is limited. Henry Kaiser, the great billionaire industrialist once commented on the magnitude of his success by suggesting simply that the key ingredient to achieving massive success in life was to "Find a need and fill it." When Dr. Covey wrote his book, entitled, The Eighth Habit: From Effectiveness to Greatness, right at the onset, he discusses the importance of addressing people's pain. Many individuals in our society are experiencing a great deal of pain. This book is just one more tool that has found its way into today's marketplace to be a means of doing just exactly what Dr. Covey speaks and writes so eloquently about.

Here are the questions I posed in that course. The responses that follow each question are from a young woman named Megan Weidig.

Question 1.

What have you learned today that will be of a significant benefit to you?

Response:

I have learned various ideas today that will impact my life. But, first, I feel that I should share a personal story with you, so you have a general idea of where I am coming from. Four months ago, I suddenly and unexpectedly lost my mother. She and I were extremely close. She was my very best friend and other half. I believe that she always wanted me to be my best and to make a caring, loving impact on others.

Now that she is physically gone, it is hard often to motivate myself. But then, I realized, she was the person who was pushing me to be my best. After taking this workshop, I have concluded that she created a desire or fire within me, and I wasn't even aware of it.

It's funny though how your thinking changes after a close and loved one is gone. I know that I have the potential and greatness within me. I know that I will succeed. I know I will make my mother proud. But, with help from this workshop, I know and I am positive that I can follow the path and achieve every one of my aspiring goals.

Question 2.

What can you do that will be of benefit to others?

Response:

Greatness is an idea that I feel anyone on the planet can accomplish. We are all human thus, we have unique feelings and emotions to express. Each person wants to do good in the world and make an impactful difference. Greatness is something I want to help others achieve. Every person desires to do great things. To do this, I will lend a helping hand, even to complete strangers to show that anyone can aspire to greatness.

Question 3

What was the best part of today's session for you?

One part of today's session that was beneficial for me was realizing that I am not the only person in the room who is afraid of succeeding. Now, that my mom is gone, I feel I have to stay at home and take care of my 14 year old sister. My father works the night shift and sometimes it is difficult to feel like a family. However, both of them encourage me constantly to go after my dreams and not hold anything back. I now realize that I am the only one holding myself back, not them or anyone else. And thank you so much Dr. Lawson for allowing me to realize this. ☺

Question 4

If I created a course on Managing Your Money Effectively, what would you want the content to focus on?

Response

One area that I plan to work on as a result of today's session is my financial issues. I have a reasonable amount of money but, I often spend it a little too quickly. From now on, I plan to place $50.00 in my savings account from each paycheck. That's $100.00 a month! Before I know it, I'll have a comfortable amount of money and will be happy and not so stressed about it.

Megan's responses are quite candid, apropos and they indicate a high level of maturity and demonstrate in written format the insights she has gained through her positive interactions with others. She has also shared with you a most intimate, amazing and incredible influence her mother has had upon her life. This incredible bond between a mother and her daughter is an inextricable link that will forever continue to shape and mold her future.

Megan's ability to articulate this clearly and share with you what motivates her is a testimony to her growing character and the positive impact she has already started to make on others. She closes her comments by making a commitment to improve her financial condition as well. When one possesses the ability to acknowledge those areas in which one needs to improve and sets a goal to accomplish it, it is that kind of a rational approach to problem solving that enables one to be a success in virtually any arena. Take a lesson from Megan. I know that I will.

The Drive to Succeed

"He who cannot save does not have the seeds of greatness within him."

W. Clement Stone

Whatever it is that you have a desire to accomplish in life, it's pretty much a proven fact that if that desire is not strong enough then, you're probably not going to accomplish your goal. An individual can possess a multitude of dynamic skills and abilities and read 100's of books all written on the subject of goal achievement, empowerment and motivation; however, unless the impetus behind what you are striving to do maintains a white hot fire that burns deep within your soul, odds are that you won't accomplish your objective.

When Lonnie Shealey penned the following quotation and disclosed it to the reading public for others to contemplate, he was indeed filled with a deep and profound insight. Take a good look at his powerful words and examine them closely. "Whatever we call it, enthusiasm, motivation, ambition, drive, desire or energy – it's a quality that plays a major role in success. People who are unable to motivate themselves must be content with mediocrity no matter how impressive their other talents."

That drive to succeed in whatever it is that you attempt to do is the one distinct quality, attribute or catalyst that serves to ignite everything else and sets you apart from the masses of people who attempt to follow in your footsteps. In this specific case, we're discussing the acquisition of money; however, this attribute can be and should be applied to whatever it is that you are pursuing.

Each individual along the pathway of life has the responsibility for defining the concept of success for himself, ferreting out exactly what he/she needs to do and then putting that specific plan into action. The decision is either an individual one or one that has been made in consultation with one's significant life partner. Once that decision has been made, then you set off on your journey of making things happen.

There are so many ways you can add fuel to your inner fire that further empowers, emboldens and drives you to succeed. Over the years, I have listened to many tapes. On one of those tapes, the very astute and savvy businessman, Jim Rohn has said on numerous occasions, that an individual can do just about anything if he has enough reasons.

Now, it's time for some contemplative and reflective thinking. You have to ask yourself a series of questions and envision how these questions can move you closer to the object of your desire.

How will your life change as a result of the additional income you will have?

Will the additional dollars provide you with a calming peace of mind?

Will you be serving as a role model for your children or someone else?

Will the increased income enable you to help yourself and others with educational expenses or other endeavors?

Will having more income than month be a difference maker?

Will the added revenue make it easier for you to establish an excellent savings and investment plan?
How will this make it possible for you to have more latitude and flexibility in your life?

Will the actions you begin taking today assist in providing a more secure financial future for you and/or your family?

This kind of a question oriented exercise helps you to comprehend the level of commitment you are planning to make to secure your own future.

By answering these questions truthfully gives you some insight into your own personality and the level of seriousness you intend to pursue in your quest to achieve financial success. The manner in which you answer each question also illustrates your level of readiness. If you are not yet ready to focus on this aspect of your life you will at least know that you are not yet ready to move forward in this area.

The initial success of the financial journey on which you are about to embark will be limited only by your attitude concerning money and your prior teachings about money that may inhibit the opportunities you have to acquire it. You may have to unlearn untruths that have literally kept some families destitute and in an impoverished state of thinking for generations. For years, in many families, backward thinking about money either through religious traditions or otherwise have kept families in financial bondage. It will be difficult to break those chains as it has been a way of life from one generation to the next.

Some individuals have conned themselves into believing that they don't' need money or that God will supply all of their needs. It is this kind of backward thinking that leads to depravity, a lack of ambition and a state of destitution. People want to help their children, put food on the table and clothes on their back yet their attitude about money is that they don't need it.

Nothing could be further from the truth. How else are they supposed to provide for themselves and/or their families? Just a few tablespoons full of commonsense should enlighten them to the fact that their own economic prowess can be a major difference maker in the quality of the life they live.

Blind piousness can play a deleterious role in one's attempt to be an economic success. Those who are victimized by religious zealots should recognize when religion is used inappropriately as a sham to discourage the average individual from seeking material wealth. In its purest sense, it is an unabashed form of mind control and a value that must be rethought or outgrown.

The point is this. Money is merely a material property than can be and should be used for constructive measures. Sharing principles with others that enables them to improve their financial lives only places them in a position where they can do more good for themselves and for others.

It was the great motivational speaker, Zig Ziglar who said, "You can get anything you want in life if you'll just help enough other people get what they want." The primary aim and purpose of this book lies in sharing a philosophy and an approach to managing finances that is designed to do exactly that.

How Doing What You Love Can Make You Rich!

"Whatever you can do or dream you can, begin it. Boldness has genius, power and magic in it."
Johann Wolfgang Von Gerte

The first time I heard these revealing words from Earl Nightingale, I was moved by them deeply. They spurred me to action. Do they do anything for you?

"If you approach one hundred individuals at the age of 25 and you ask them if they would like to be wealthy in the field of their choice, you will notice a sparkle in their eye and an eagerness toward life and yet if you project these same individuals 40 years into the future to the age of 65 and you allow for growth, opportunity, time and experience. In the richest nation on earth, here is what you will find. Only one will be wealthy, four will be financially independent, 30 of them will be dead and the remaining 65 will be forced to rely upon government programs to survive their remaining years of life."

There are essentially two primary reasons why this is so. One is that people conform to what society says is right for them instead of marching to the beat of their own drummer. The second reason quite simply is that people do not set goals.

I cannot adequately put into words how excited I am about writing this chapter because it contains the very heart and essence of success. Once you have finished this chapter, if you are able to digest its content and apply these principles directly to your life you will be well on your way to creating your own fortune. Before I share that information, however, I want to provide you with another eye opening stat that just might grab your attention. Out of all the individuals who read books, attend, seminars, conferences and workshops or courses, only 8% of those individuals rarely put any of the information to use. Clearly 92% of the individuals in question close the book when they are finished with it or leave the seminar or course to get their credit and life for them continues on pretty much the way it always did before they read the book or went to the course. That's kind of a shame isn't it? Why waste the professor's time? Why waste the author's time? More importantly, why waste your own? Why? Why? Why? Seriously contemplate these ideas just for a moment. That's all I ask. Does this make any sense? You cannot continue to do the same things that you are currently and expect to get different results. The only time that things change for you is when you change things. Another thing that I like to tell people is that they should be 100% wherever they are. Here's the point. If you are in attendance at a lecture or a seminar, don't' spend time day dreaming. If you are a captive for eight hours of instruction, make the most of it and see what you can learn. You might acquire some extremely beneficial information that will enable you to make significant progress in your life.

This is powerful stuff! Alan Loy McGinnis wrote a book entitled *The Confidence Factor*. In the book, he mentions a study that was conducted on 1500 men and women who were followed for 20 years. Of those 1500, 83 became millionaires. There were interesting characteristics that stood out in these folks.

They had not set out to be wealthy; that happened as a by-product of what they were doing.

The secret, if there was a secret was, they decided to specialize and do something that absorbed them totally—something they loved to do. And in specializing and doing what they loved to do over the years, they became very good at it. As a result, they were paid well.

They also had another characteristic. They didn't throw money around as many of the others had. They invested carefully. After 15-20 years of hard work, they lifted up their heads and discovered their net worth was well over a million. They were so busy being excellent at what they were doing that they were hardly aware of how wealthy they were becoming. And the interesting thing is, they weren't entrepreneurs or great technical geniuses. Seventy to eighty per cent of them worked for a salaried company. There are two keys that are critical to making this process work.

1. Assess your skills and determine where you can make a contribution.

2. Practice and become exceptionally good at this particular endeavor.

Now, research adequately illustrates that there's an effective way for us to get this done. Why should we reinvent the wheel when all we have to do is apply the principles that we know will work. Here they are.

Yale University – 1953 --3% of graduating seniors completed all 7 steps of a goal setting program. An additional 10% took 5 of the steps. 87% beyond identifying what they wanted to be hadn't taken any of the steps. In 1973—20 years later, they conducted another study and here's what they found. The 3% who had taken all of the steps had clearly accomplished more than the 97% who had not.

Now, obviously, there are several things we have to know and understand. Firstly, on the goal achievement process, there are four primary reasons why people are so unable to achieve the desires of their heart and/or whatever it is that they covet so much.

1. They've been told but they've never been sold.
2. Don't know how
3. Fear of failure
4. Poor Self Image

So then, even if you never decided to put any of the seven steps of the goal achievement plan to work, wouldn't you at least want to know what they were? Here they are.

1. Identify your goal.
2. Set a deadline for its achievement.
3. Determine the obstacles that impede your progress.
4. Decide what gifts, talents, skills or abilities you will need.
5. Decide who's going to work with you.
6. Develop an action plan.
7. Prepare to enjoy the benefits.

The development of the action plan is perhaps one of the most critical components of the goal achievement strategy because it demonstrates the commitment level and the serious intent of its owner. The action in essence becomes the roadmap of your ultimate objective.

Henriette Ann Klauser in her best selling book, *Write It Dowm; Make It Happen* illustrates the importance of such an idea just by the title of her masterpiece. Dr. Stephen Covey, the author of the 8th Habit and numerous other books validates the importance of getting things down on paper and illustrates the scientific merits of such a bonafide action by virtue of this quote.

"Even more powerful than visualization, writing bridges the conscious and the subconscious mind; writing is a psycho neuro muscular activity that literally imprints the brain. To test this, before you go to bed, write down what you want to do or think about first thing in the morning and just see what happens. In almost all cases, you will have a consciousness of those things when you wake up in the morning."

Another one of my favorite authors, Dr. Wayne Dyer in his most recent book, *Excuses Begone,* discusses the scarcity mentality that most people possess versus the abundance mentality which they should be pursuing. Here's one of the things he says, "When you say, "I love my job but I'll never get rich at it", "You are aligning yourself with a frequency (energy) that will give you what you think."

Instead of buying into that particular thinking paradigm we should shift our focus and hone in on what we intend to create. Dr Dyer goes on to say this, "By believing that the universe is all-providing and by knowing that I'm worthy of the unlimited beneficence of the Source of Being, I just keep attracting prosperity to me." I must tell you that I totally buy Dr. Dyer's argument.

My thinking is aligned with his in the sense that I think we as human beings should develop an incredible "attitude of gratitude" by being thankful for everything we have in life. Not what we lack but what we have. The more we can illustrate our thankfulness from a genuine and sincere perspective in terms of the very breath we breathe, the jobs we have, the time that's left – all place us in an abundance mentality mode that enables us to align ourselves with a far more potent energy source that allows us to attract more into our lives instead of less. What an incredible and powerful lesson for those who are in tune with the spiritual realm and believe this. This is the kind of powerful thinking that literally enables you to manifest your destiny.

As Dr. Dyer might say, you have accepted the responsibility for your own life by taking charge of your thoughts and creating the future you desire by virtue of the actions you've chosen to take in the present moment.

Consider this statement, "There is no force in the world that has a greater impact than the statement of a knowledgeable person fortified by confidence and experience. An individual who knows and knows that he knows can speak with authority that has no comparison. The world makes way for the man or woman who knows what he is doing."

Take the time to purposefully analyze every aspect of the passage you just read and you will immediately see why it is so phenomenal. Ponder on it for a moment. Examine it carefully. There should be no question as to why this is one of the primary secrets to achieving financial success or any other kind of success for that matter.

Let me illustrate if I may in the simplest terms I know. If I tell you that I have $5,000 in the bank, $10,000 in the bank or $15,000 for that matter, whatever the denomination is, is real for me. And, if I have disciplined myself over the years to save and invest, whatever the denomination is, then I essentially have expert proof that I have the ability to generate a certain amount of revenue. Guess what? Once I have proven to myself that I have the ability to do that, what can stop me from replicating that process again and again and again until such time that I have finally achieved the economic goal that I have set for myself? And don't forget the multiplication factor or exponential reality that becomes a part of this process with your forward movement that accelerates your results.

When I speak to others then about the issue of money, it bolsters my credibility because I know that for me this is a certainty. It dons the persona of something more powerful than a thought or a belief because it is a knowing. It transcends all else because it is an actual manifestation as a result of those things.

Dare to Be a Millionaire

The Power of Focus

"Man was designed for accomplishment, engineered for success and endowed with the seeds of greatness."

Zig Ziglar

It was the great Og Mandino, author of *The Greatest Salesman in the World* who once said, "Many of us never realize our greatness because we become sidetracked by secondary activity." In other words, we lose our focus.

Whatever it is that you so strongly and so ardently desire must become the centralizing focal point of your thought process. The more you are able to focus and direct your energy, your time, your effort, your abilities, your talents and your skills on doing the very things at which you excel, the more successful you will become.

This tremendous power of concentrated effort and focus is the very thing that will assist you in generating the kind of revenue for which you are looking. As you get to a certain point in your life and start to reflect on what you have been able to achieve, you will immediately note that your greatest achievements occurred during those moments when you were at the very height of your intense power of concentration and focus.

As Og Mandino's quote at the very beginning of this chapter implies, the more effective you become at dealing with life's distractions, the sooner you will be able to achieve your financial objectives. Learn to work hard and smart and learn to do it continuously day in and day out.

Dr. John Maxwell, author of the *Twenty – One Irrefutable Laws of Leadership* and over 100 additional books once made this astute observation. "One is too small a number to achieve greatness." This is a most powerful and insightful truth. Whatever it is that you have a desire to share must not only have tremendous value for you; it must also be highly beneficial to others as well. The more beneficial, meaningful and noteworthy it is to others, the greater will be its profitability for you.

One of the major keys that contributes significantly to an individual's financial success lies in making sure that those within your sphere of influence become even more cognizant of the abilities, talents and skills that you have to offer so that they can be utilized as effectively as they possibly can by many others. This is one of the key laws of success that works to perfection.

If you know precisely how to do something extraordinarily well and you possess the ability to share that knowledge with others, you are in essence destined for greatness far beyond the capacity of your own limited imagination. You can literally write the book on success. People will want what you've got.

You must perfect your craft and be able to demonstrate and illustrate the significant and positive impact that it produces in the lives of others. Once you have done that, then you must promote your unique selling proposition in a manner that maximizes its potential.

You must do this by boldly and unabashedly utilizing every potential resource that is available to you. The greatest marketing tool that I currently have at my disposal is word of mouth. My students have not only been one of my top sources of inspiration; they have also been my greatest promoters. I have lost count of the numerous times that I have heard someone say that they bought one of my books or attended one of my lectures, seminars, conferences, workshops or courses simply because they were referred by someone else. There is no higher recommendation or compliment in life than that of a satisfied customer, client, patron, acquaintance or friend. One who has a direct experience can speak with a frankness and a conviction that is virtually unmatched.

Your ability to network effectively with others can aid you in creating an infrastructure that can literally propel you into the limelight and place you at the top of your profession faster than anything you could have dreamed possible. Individuals who can do many things well are sometimes at a distinct disadvantage because they have a propensity for wanting to be all things to all people.

Their numerous talents are almost a curse because their ability to do so many things well neutralizes their ability to focus and concentrate on the one thing that could propel them into an arena where they could enjoy massive success. Oftentimes, they end up sacrificing the great accomplishment for that of the good.

Those individuals who are the most successful in our society are those individuals who have learned through trial and error, hard work, luck, perseverance, setbacks and various other types of circumstances what their primary purpose in life is. They have also learned specifically how to focus their time, their energy and their efforts on that specific purpose in an attempt to achieve maximum results.

In the end, they are able to achieve their ultimate objective simply because they refused to quit, give up, or throw in the towel. Their amazing, incredible and enduring tenacity is the one quality that enables them to overcome every adversity and every obstacle thrown in their path. Not everyone possesses that quality but those individuals who do are destined to reap powerful rewards as a gift for their refusal to quit. The power of focus must not be underestimated. It is a gift that elevates champions above the masses of people who aspire to be like them.

How Wealthy People Think

"Perhaps the most valuable result of all education is the ability to make yourself do the thing you have to do, when it ought to be done, whether you like it or not."
Thomas Huxley

Why reinvent the wheel? If the formula for creating a wealth mentality has already been written about, why not secure those books that show you what to do and start applying those principles to your own life? Not only is Dr. Charles J. Stanley a visionary, he is also an astute researcher and a brilliant thinker who has carved out a path which you can emulate once you get to the point where you understand it.

In his fascinating book, *The Millionaire Mind*, the research he has unearthed reveals a number of key ideas that are beneficial to helping people become financially independent. He immediately identifies four extraneous variables that impact significantly the acquisition of wealth process. They are as follows:

- Loving your work and being excited about it daily

- Knowing that your chosen vocation is one that allows full use of your abilities and aptitudes

- Getting high self esteem from your work

- Being absolutely certain that your vocation will make you financially independent one day

If such is the case then you should have no difficulty focusing on your goal and working at a high level of productivity. The reason that so few people are financially independent today is that they place many negative roadblocks in their head. Becoming wealthy is in fact a mind game. It is as Napoleon Hill said in his masterpiece, *Think and Grow Rich*, "Whatever the mind can conceive and believe, it can achieve."

Before you can become a millionaire, you must learn to think like one. You must learn how to motivate yourself constantly to counter fear with courage.

Dr. Stanley says, "All this revolves around your becoming a collector of data and information that have value if they are concentrated. As I said in my last chapter, too many people lack focus. They are not collectors of anything. Not data, not customers, not specific marketable skills. On the other hand, collectors can read one newspaper and find several ideas or pieces of information about their chosen vocation. In twenty years they can generate a collection of treasure." These words and two powerful lists that follow are extracted directly from Charles J. Stanley's book.

Notice an underlying theme in this passage that validates the point that becoming wealthy is not an overnight process. Dr. Stanley mentions what individuals can generate in twenty years through their diligence in collecting ideas they can act on. That is precisely why this book is based on the twenty year concept.

In the *Millionaire Mind*, Dr. Stanley identifies thirteen key characteristics that are generally portrayed by wealthy people. They are as follows:

1. Being honest with all people.

2. Having a supportive spouse.

3. Getting along with people.

4. Loving my career/business.

5. Being physically fit.

6. Having strong leadership qualities.

7. Making wise investments.

8. Seeing business opportunities others did not see.

9. Being willing to take financial risks given the right return.

10. Having good mentors.

11. Investing in my own business.

12. Living below my means.

13. Having excellent investment advisers.

Dr. Stanley goes on to explain that "Eighty-two percent of America's millionaires are first generation. Affluent people typically follow a lifestyle conducive to accumulating money."

He identifies seven specific beliefs or actions that they take.

Here they are. See how closely your thinking is aligned with theirs and if not, what it will take to get you there.

1. They live well below their means.

2. They allocate their time, energy and money efficiently in ways conducive to building wealth.

3. They believe their financial independence is more important than displaying high social status.

4. Their parents did not provide economic outpatient care.

5. Their adult children are economically self sufficient.

6. They are proficient in targeting market opportunities.

7. They chose the right occupation.

Growing Your Wealth

"It is in your moments of decision that your destiny is shaped."

Anthony Robbins

Making critical decisions about your career, business, investments and other resources is what conjures up fear or that which is a natural part of becoming a financial success.

One Specific Approach

1. **Saving -- Proving to yourself that you can do it!**
   a. **discipline**
   b. **focus**

2. **CD's**

3. **Establish a great relationship with a personal banker.**

4. **Investment Specialist**

5. **Diversified Portfolio**

Right now, your earnings are coming from what you have the ability to currently generate. You should take all of what is shared into consideration, step back, look at the big picture in the grand scheme of things and ask yourself this question. What works best for me and the situation I am currently in? We all have to do that because we are individuals and what works well for one person may not work well for the next. There

is not one specific magic formula that works well for all people. The only things that are guaranteed are these, death, taxes and the fact that if we continue to do what we have always done, we will continue to get what we have always gotten.

Now, if we are satisfied with that then, I suppose that's ok. But, if we are not, ok with that then it stands to reason that we should make a few changes in our lifestyles and how we are currently handling our finances so that the lot that we currently have can be turned into a lot more.

In order for that to happen, we need to think in terms of four critical areas. I use an acronym to keep it simple. Here it is.

a. Earning

b. Saving

c. Investing

d. Eliminating debt

In other words, it's **EASY**   **(ESIE)** ☺

A Case Study of A Teacher and a Lawyer

"Self control and self discipline are both attributes of true freedom because discipline is self imposed law. This is freedom."

Dr. Myles Monroe

In the *Millionaire Mind*, Thomas J. Stanley, Ph.D. and William D. Danko, Ph.D. share a case study about two brothers. One is a teacher and the other is an attorney. Both brothers are raised in a prominent and well to do millionaire household. Both education and money are treated with a great deal of respect.

You can give these brothers any names you want to, but, the point that both authors have a desire to make with their reading audience is most profound. Most outside observers would automatically think that one who becomes an attorney in the family would most logically be the one to make more money and manage it more effectively as well.

Regarding wealth accumulation, the teacher's total household income for the year was $71,000. His brother's household income was $123,000. As the authors point out, the attorney's income is nearly twice that of his brother's. However, there are key rules that one must consider and adhere to when it comes to building wealth.

Although the teacher earns a considerably lower salary, he handles his finances much differently than does his brother. Firstly, he doesn't live above his means. On the other hand, the attorney is far more consumer oriented and status driven than he is oriented towards saving money and producing wealth. His focus is more on the accumulation of things. As a result of this tendency towards self-indulgence, the attorney's net worth is $553,000 and his brother, the teacher's net worth is $834,000.

The authors point out that "as a group, teachers are more frugal." The difference in the outcome relates specifically to their respective positions and their attitudes towards wealth building. Regardless of an individual's societal position, those who spend less and focus more on saving and investing opportunities will always have substantially more income.

This case study really does provide an amazing and incredible amount of hope for the average person. It adds more fuel to the old adage, "It's not how much you make. It's what you do with what you make." Any individual who has the desire to become wealthy in one generation must have the ability to develop the courage to offset the fear of economic failure.

Budgetary Assessment: What Action Steps Can I Take Today?

1. Pay down credit card bills/ Eliminate Debt.

2. A Part of all I earn is mine to keep/ Start paying myself first.

3. Look for additional opportunities to make money.

    a. Earning Money – job, part time job, business, etc

    b.   Savings Account

    c.   Investing Money

    d.   Eliminating Debt

4. Follow up – Follow Through.

5. Read about successful people and replicate what they do on a manageable scale as it applies to your situation.

6. Attend success oriented and money management seminars and apply the principles you learn.

7. Think and Act Positively.

Getting Your Debt Under Control

> "Well done is better than well said."
>
> Benjamin Franklin

If you have multiple credit cards, occasionally you can apply for others that carry lower interest rates. This simply means that if you are wise, prudent and disciplined, you can have your balances transferred from cards that carry high interest rates to those with much lower rates. This is one idea that can help you start the slow process to financial recovery.

In one instance, I had one card on which the interest rate was a whopping 24%. Implementing this change enabled me to reduce my interest charges by almost 50%. The new card's rate was 12.99%. Established lending companies looking to expand their customer base sometimes offer zero interest incentives on balance transfers. They don't mind taking on customers with additional debt if those customers have a good track record of meeting their monthly payments on a regular basis.

The alert consumer has to be on the lookout for opportunities that may arise that will enable them to resolve their debt obligations more quickly in order to secure more of their earned income for savings and investment purposes. The sooner you can turn your outgo into income, the more advantageous it is going to be for you.

Pay more attention to the fine print on your credit cards that arrive on your doorstep each month. Under the guidance of the Obama Administration, two things have happened that are critical to customer or card holders of lending companies.

(1). Currently, your credit card statements are arriving a week earlier than they had been previously. The purpose of this extra time provides you with a built in cushion to figure out what else you can do before the due date of your payment arrives.

(2). If you read the fine print, you will note the length of time it will take you to pay off your current balance if you continue to make the minimum payment. Also listed is an alternative figure and pay off date that illustrates how much you can save if you can improve your financial condition to the point where you can send the company more than the minimum payment. This savings is substantial and the money you save as you already know is hard earned money that you can now redirect to your own account and suddenly, money that was flowing out of your home in such an insipid manner starts flowing in. Your outgo becomes your income and that is exactly what we want. Let's examine closely four specific scenarios to see how this works.

(Scenario 1)

Let's say you have a credit card and the minimum monthly payment that you are sending in is $209.00 per month. This is to satisfy a balance of over $10,000. In five years, you will have paid out $13,444.64. If you got to the point where you could send in $324.00 each month, you could pay the balance off in 3 years or 36 months. This would result in a savings of $2,000.00 which could be deposited into your savings or investment account. The annual percentage rate of your card is 12.99.

(Scenario 2)

You have a card that has a balance of $9,137.21. The minimum payment you are making is $146.48. If the interest rate for the lending company is 19.99 %, at this rate, it will take you 23 years to pay off the debt and you will have paid them a total of $14,190.00. If you could manage to increase your minimum payment to $283.00 per month, you could have the balance paid off in 3 years and save an estimated $4,000 by reducing the overall amount of interest on your debt to $10,192.00.

(Scenario 3)

Having a card that has an interest rate of 21.24 per cent and a balance you owe of $5,880.82 where you are making a minimum payment of $118.00 means that you will end up paying out $11,979.00 over a 17 year period in order to settle the debt. If you could somehow get yourself into a position where you could manage to send in $188.00 a month over a three year period, you could end your debt liability and save $6,771.00. You must simply ask yourself this question. Is it worth it? Do you prefer to pay $118.00 for 17 years or $188.00 for three? Here's another question. If you are going to pay $118.00 for the next 17 years, shouldn't it be to yourself?

(Scenario 4)

The fourth scenario is where you are currently making a minimum payment of $82.00 per month and the interest rate on your card is 24%. If you continue to send in the minimum payment, it will take 20 years to pay off the debt. That's $8, 225.12. It doesn't look like much but, the payment seems to go on perpetually because of the high interest rate. If you could get to the point where you could pay $140.28 for 3 years, you would in essence pay $5,050.59 and save $3,175.03 and have the debt resolved.

The bottom line is simply this. The faster you can take the extra money that you earn and apply it to your debt, the sooner you will be able to ease the financial burden that is eating away at your income.

If these tips, strategies and ideas are not enough to help you return to the road of financial solvency, you certainly have other options that you can exercise or explore. In those areas where you have little or no expertise, I urge you to proceed with caution and acquire advice from experts in the field of finance. For example, if you are considering working with a debt consolidation company, check with others to see how well it has worked for them. Find out the track record of the company with which you are planning to get involved. Just because the company has taken the time to get an endorsement from some movie star that you've recognized in movies over the years and have a deep admiration for does not mean that what this company does will work for you. Nor does it exonerate them from what may have happened to other customers who worked with them. Horror stories abound. There's always another price to pay for something that on the surface looks to good to be true. It probably is.

Perhaps the most devastating thing to do would be to set up a payment arrangement, go against all of the principles you've been taught over the years, go in business with a company you know nothing about and then have that company to go out of business because of poor performance, questionable tactics and still have to end up paying off your old debt in addition to the money you sent the company to get your debt problems resolved in the first place. That's called a double whammy. God knows you do not deserve that. What a financial nightmare that would be. Statistics show that 75% of these companies fail.

Though I have never done it myself, I do know that when things look absolutely horrific, filing for bankruptcy can be another option. Numerous books are written on the topic and the rules vary from state to state. Be sure to explore the bankruptcy concept thoroughly before making a decision to follow through on it. That's the soundest advice I know how to give. You need to see first hand how your situation will be affected, how long it will take you to recover from such an action and how long your credit will be affected. Both your credit rating and your ability to borrow money from others could possibly be hampered or jeopardized for quite some time.

Though I am not an authority on bankruptcy or debt consolidation companies, the one thing I do know for certain is this. The principles we are discussing in this book on saving and investing money do work and that much I can guarantee 100%. Here's the catch. In order for the principles to work, you have to work the principles. The only other thing I advise people to do in each instance where they are about to make a decision that affects their finances either negatively or positively is to consult with someone who is highly skilled or knowledgeable in each arena.

Consult with those individuals who know precisely what they are doing by virtue of their educational background and training in the field or by virtue of their direct experience. Certified Public Accountants Certified Financial Planners, investment specialists, personal bankers and reputable tax establishments are five that initially come to mind. Provide them with an opportunity to assist you in establishing the kind of plan that will enable you to yield the highest rate of return on your investment. That is exactly what I did and that is exactly what I am continuing to do. It works.

Another strategy you can use to curtail your debt or get it under control is by making a conscientious effort not to incur any additional debt. Like the insurance companies suggest, "Life comes at you fast." None of us is exempt from encountering unexpected events that occur in our lives and catch us completely off guard. Before you know it, there you are right in the middle of spending even more dollars while you're still struggling to resolve the debt you already have. It seems there's no end in sight. If I sound a bit empathetic, it's because I've experienced it directly.

This is precisely why your ability to save becomes even more important. While you are trying to pay down your debt that carries high interest rates, even though it doesn't seem or sound plausible to save, you must. Why? Because you benefit in the long run especially if you have enough cash saved to offset any additional debt you might incur. That might include educational expenses for children in college, your home unexpectedly being burglarized, hitting a deer with your car, having to purchase a new vehicle. Let's face it. Just because we have debt doesn't mean that life comes to a grinding halt. It is quite the contrary.

Life goes on. So, if you have enough cash on hand to settle upcoming expenses, how wonderful it becomes for you not to have to add those expenses to your existing debt. Because of the disciplined habit you have finally cultivated to save, you can now start getting ahead.

The Power of Compound Interest

"Apply yourself to any course marked out for yourself industriously, punctually and persistently, and you prevail. Having this marvelous power at command, use it!"
William James Tilley

Regardless of what age people are who attend the seminars that I conduct or the books, CD's or other products I produce, one of the most important things I want them to fully understand is the power of compound interest and how they can make it work for them. The sooner they get started on building their financial nest egg, the better. If you are a twenty something or a thirty something, there is great hope for you. If you are a sixty something like me, you can still get it done but time is running out. In fact, when I listen to the Adam Bohl mutual fund show and hear a seventy something or an eighty something getting all excited about money they have invested and what they can do to move it around a little to maximize their returns even more, I get inspired all over again. You see, until they put you in a pine box, it's never too late so regardless of your age, keep on truckin.

One of the most powerful articles I've ever seen written on the subject, I discovered when I was on the internet. It was written by Kenneth Petersen. It can be a life changing experience for those who truly get it. Someone actually wrote in, made a statement and then asked a question. This is how it went.

Several years ago, you wrote an article about the power of compound interest. You used the example of two girls just out of college. One started saving right away and the other didn't. The one that waited never caught up. Could you tell me again how that worked?

In their new book *The Elements of Investing*, Burton G. Malkiel and Charles D. Ellis devote the entire first chapter to the importance of saving. In a section titled "Start Saving Early – Time is Money" they offer these words of wisdom" The secret of getting rich slowly but surely is the miracle of compound interest. Albert Einstein is said to have described compound interest as the most powerful force in the universe."

If you follow my story about young women just out of college, you will understand what Einstein meant. Hannah and Lilly are not just best friends. They both graduated from college and celebrated their 22nd birthday last year on the same day.

After a summer of fun, they started work in September. On her 22nd birthday, Hannah put $3,000 into a Roth IRA account. She continues to put $3,000 into her account on her birthday for 10 years, until she turns 31. After that she doesn't contribute another dime. Lilly, who makes the same income as Hannah, loves to shop. She never has any money left over to save.

On their 31st birthday, Hannah tells Lilly that her Roth IRA is now worth $46,936. Hannah also tells Lilly that she is now making house payments and will not be able to make any more contributions to her IRA.

Lilly, a competitive type, sees her chance to catch up to Hannah and starts saving. She opens a Roth IRA and sends in her first check for $3,000.

Every year Lilly sends in another $3,000 and every year the two get together on their birthday. The first thing Lilly always asks Hannah is 'How much is your IRA worth today?" And every year Lilly learns that Hannah's IRA is still bigger. For 34 years, Lilly adds $3,000 to her Roth IRA and Hannah contributes nothing.

And every year for 34 years when they meet, Lilly learns that she hasn't caught up. When they meet to celebrate their 65th birthday, they compare Roth IRA accounts. Hannah has $642,560 of tax free money, $128, 610 more than Lilly, who has $513,950.

Hannah's total contributions were only $30,000. Lilly contributed $102,000 ($72,000 more than Hannah) and never caught up. That's the power of compound interest.

What if Hannah had continued to contribute until she was 65, instead of stopping at age 31? Her contributions would have totaled $132,000 and her account would be worth almost $1.2 million, all tax free. As Ben Franklin said, "money makes money and the money that money makes makes money."

Tracking Your Dollars Makes Cents/Sense

"Until thought is linked with purpose, there is no intelligent accomplishment."
James Allen

One of the primary tools that one must use to improve one's financial position is a budgetary data analysis. To determine better in what direction you are headed, it's imperative to get a better handle on where you've been financially, a firm grip on where you are and a clear and precise idea on where you want to go.

If you know what your monthly expenses are, it better enables you to determine how much you can afford and you have an immediate picture of how much debt you have and how long it's going to take you to pay it off so that it can no longer maintain the stranglehold it has on your income and your ability to produce additional revenue. For those of you who have no debt, that is absolutely fantastic. It just puts you that much further ahead in the financial game of life and provides you with a wonderful opportunity to invest a portion of your income in those areas that are most beneficial for your own financial growth.

The more debt that one has, the more debilitating and crippling its effect when one sees that continuing loss on a monthly basis.

The sooner that one can eliminate as much debt as possible, the more one can contribute towards both a savings and an investment plan. The sooner that you can start the investment process, the more economic advantages you will have and the more revenue generating strategies you can apply earlier in life.

Obviously, you do not have to wait until you are completely out of debt to start an excellent savings and investment plan. In fact, when you are doing more for yourself than you are doing right now, sometimes, you begin to see the error of your previous ways and it spurs you to start making better economic decisions more quickly and eliminating the debt that has held you captive for years.

This is precisely why having and maintaining a budget is very beneficial in so many ways. When you have a budget, for example, and an opportunity arises where you might consider spending money frivolously, you may rethink that decision and keep those dollars because of your budgetary limitation. It gives a completely new meaning to the Clint Eastwood phrase, "A man has got to know his limitations." Mission accomplished. Money saved. It's that simple.

You may avoid incurring additional debt simply because you are in a financial position to do so. This can be a blessing in disguise and a benefit in helping you to realize your financial goals faster. The amount of money that people can consume or expend in a lifetime is just staggering.

What could they do and how much money would they have to do so if they could develop the discipline necessary to reverse the general tendency to spend and focus their efforts on saving and investing instead? Be sure to read and reread the chapter on the power of compound interest. That chapter provides you with amazing insights on ways you can start getting your money to work for you.

Not only can you build an amazing and financial legacy but over a period of twenty years or so you can position yourself to spend money arbitrarily without too much of a negative effect. What a wonderful position to be in.

Having and maintaining a budget and living below your means which is one of the major characteristics for prodigious accumulators of wealth can place you in a position of economic power. For anyone who desires to achieve financial freedom, discipline is essential.

If you maintain a chart of your outgoing expenses on a monthly basis, you will have an immediate picture or vision of how much you owe your creditors. If it is initially overwhelming and depressing, you can also create a chart that shows your income, savings, retirement and other figures that are illustrative of the progress you are making as you move closer to achieving your financial goals. Obviously, you will want to include your monthly salary and any other earnings you have. This budgetary visual organizer can help you to lay out your expenses as well as your income in such a fashion that you can begin to prioritize your debts and see which ones you can get paid off the soonest. Select one and make it a primary goal to eliminate it completely. Each time you do that, not only are you eliminating the debt but you are also eliminating any unnecessary interest payments that go to your creditors. All of those dollars that were going out to others will now remain in your pocket to be used for more constructive things if you so choose. Your ability to concentrate and focus on paring down these economic vermin in their entirety just eliminates one more financial burden that is weighing heavily upon your mind.

Here's a word of caution. Don't stress out over the total amount you owe. You didn't acquire those bills overnight so, it's not totally realistic to think that they will all disappear tomorrow.

However, if you have incurred a mountain of debt, you can alleviate it in the same manner in which it was created. In fact, there's an old Chinese proverb that states the following:

"He who would remove a mountain must begin by taking away small stones." Most folks at one time or another have felt as though they've been buried under a mountain of debt and that someone was also cruel enough to bury the earth movers right along with them (Ha). It saps your energy and makes you feel that when you're working, you're just spinning your wheels and not making any progress.

Regardless of how steep the climb might be, if you possess the discipline, the drive and the determination to get out of debt, you can and you will succeed. If I write this as though I have experienced a minute portion of what some people are going through, it's because I have. The personal experiences I've had with money are what have provided the impetus for me to write this book.

When you have a budget that you can review at will on a periodic basis, it helps you to keep your own mind's decision making apparatus in a fully functional mode and when you think about incurring additional debt, a red flag or a warning will go off inside your head and hopefully, you will refrain from impulse purchasing and doing further harm to your financial life.

When an individual reviews his budgetary data, it is incumbent upon him to make a conscientious effort to include a category for those irregular expenses that one incurs periodically. For example, car insurance and property taxes are not generally extracted from a person's paycheck on a monthly basis; however, if one forgets about those outlandish expenses and doesn't consider them a part of one's budgetary planning purpose, can you not see how quickly that kind of on the spur of the moment capital outlay can throw a financial monkey wrench into the amount of money you thought you were going to have for that particular month? This is just one more reason why budgeting is a good idea.

Though I have alluded to this next situation in another part of the book, I will mention it briefly here as well. Those emergency expenses that occur can be a major impediment to a person's positive cash flow. When you can, prepare for those doctor visits that are least expected, those dentist visits, automobile repairs, funeral expenses etc. If one gets into a position to be more accommodating to these irregularities, it lessens the frustration and strain on your budget and keeps you in a state of perpetual, forward motion.

For those individuals who do not have the discipline to save for these kinds of emergencies, many corporations, businesses, educational institutions and social service organizations have employee medical plans where you can have money set aside from your paycheck and placed in a designated medical account strictly to cover health related issues. Your becoming an active participant in this kind of a plan can only be beneficial to you in the long run.

One of the most important things to consider when you are reviewing your budgetary data is that if things have really spun out of control and you need professional, financial counseling, there are experts who can analyze your data and assist you in assembling a plan of action that will enable you to re-evaluate and reorganize your financial situation and get you back on track. One phone call to a certified financial planner could do the job in helping you to reorganize your finances, pay down debt and put you back in control of your money. The first step lies in admitting that you need help.

Over the years, I've read books, watched T.V. programs, listened to radio commentary, and searched the internet in an attempt to resolve my own financial dilemmas. Ironically, what I have learned is that no one is exempt from encountering financial difficulties. One of the things that has stunned me the most is listening to financial advisers and gurus in the finance industry who've had to own up to the fact that there were times in their lives where they too had to discover a good solution to an existing financial problem they had. I suppose the real eye opener for me was learning that even individuals who had given tons of financial advice and had even written books on the topic were they themselves victims of financial exigency.

Honor Your Gift

"A man's gift maketh room for him and bringeth him before great men."

Proverbs 18:16

The fifth book of the Bible, Deuteronomy the 8th Chapter and the 18th verse begins in this manner. "But remember the Lord your God for it is He who gives you the ability to produce wealth and so confirms his covenant which He swore to your forefathers as it is today."

What talents, gifts, skills or abilities has God hidden in your heart? When was the last time you felt so strongly about something you knew you just had to do? Many times in life, individuals can feel the great Spirit urging them to move in the direction of their destiny and they second guess that passionate urging and resist the temptation to follow it.

Then, sometime later in life, they take stock of themselves, their surroundings in life and they wonder why they feel so dissatisfied. It is because they have not yet aligned themselves with their true purpose in life. Perhaps out of necessity or because of a lack of faith or belief in the gifts they possess, they have just simply not pursued their ultimate calling.

Stephen Prefontaine, the great distance runner whose life was tragically cut short by a car accident at the age of 24 once made this statement. "To give anything less than your best is to sacrifice the gift." These are indeed some extremely powerful words, not to mention the fact that they display an advanced wisdom of one so young.

In previous years, I have had the distinct honor and privilege of working with one of America's top professional speakers and businessmen, Harvey Alston. Mr. Alston is unequivocally one of the best empowerment speakers in the world as well as one of the most economically savvy. He has spoken in every state of the continental United States as well as in numerous international countries. Watching him hone his skills and polish his craft over the years and then use it to inspire millions of people around the world to improve their lives is a miraculous event to behold. Spreading hope to millions of others and providing them with a higher degree of self confidence as well as the skills and the tools they need that gets them to believe more fully in themselves is honoring your gift. That, my friends, is honoring your gift.

Another business friend of mine, Ella Coleman, is the publisher of *Purpose Magazine*. I once wrote a cover story for her featuring Harvey Alston. That was back in 1996. During that year, Mr. Alston picked the shortest month of the year, February, in which to deliver 61 presentations and earn in compensation for his services for that one month, a figure totaling $45,000.00. That is a figure that many folks still are unable to amass in one year.

Now, I am well aware of the fact that there are individuals like Colin Powell, for example, or Laura Bush, who can earn upwards of $60,000 plus for one engagement. However, keep in mind that these individuals have achieved celebrity status. They are known all over the world. Harvey Alston, on the other hand, is a self made millionaire who might walk into a school system and speak to a group of students for as little as $800 - $1500. Imagine the energy it must take to do that over and over and over to generate a figure of $45,000.00.

At Georgetown Jr-Sr. High School, in Georgetown, Ohio in addition to English and poetry classes, I sometimes teach an elective course to high school students on leadership. For one assignment, I had my students to read the magazine article that I had written on Mr. Alston.

My students were so inspired and so impressed with Mr. Alston's ability to share and his economic success that they decided to write him a letter to let him know how positively he had impacted their lives through his powerful message and his selflessness.

A few weeks after I sent Mr. Alston the letters from my students, he surprised them by responding. He sent a letter thanking the students for their support and praising them for getting an education to help not only themselves but others. As a former educator and college graduate himself, Mr. Alston knows the value of an education and the options it affords others in today's society. Mr. Alston has an incredible ability and an innate gift in connecting with others and the education he has obtained has been a key component in his rise to the top of his profession.

Mr. Alston thoroughly enjoys interacting with students around the world as well as educators and business people as he moves from educational institutions, businesses, industries and corporations to deliver his powerful message.

Before I tell you how he ends his riveting and high-energy packed programs, let me also tell you about a movie called the Guardian in which Kevin Costner and Ashton Kutcher play significant roles.

Their characters meet when Kevin Costner (Ben Randall) is sent by his commanding officer to take a break from the high intense drama and pace that he is used to when the character he plays (Randall) appears to be mentally shaken and distraught after a failed rescue attempt. Costner's character (Randall) is sent to a training school to teach a young group of coast guard upstarts how to become rescue swimmers.

Here, he encounters Ashton Kutcher (Jake Fischer) who portrays a highly competitive youth and obviously needs to learn a few things about selflessness. His somewhat combative personality can partially be attributed to his high level of confidence and the fact that his overachieving is compensating for some unknown event that transpired earlier in his life which is being masked.

At any rate, these two characters survive their initial challenge and establish a bond that at first seems unlikely to transpire. It is in this movie that a powerful line emerges. When Ashton Kutcher (Jake Fischer) encounters some difficult decisions he has to make concerning life choices, Kevin Costner (Ben Randall's) character emerges on the scene and says simply, "Honor your gift." That is probably one of the most powerful lines in the movie akin to Robin Williams (Professor Keating) in the movie, The Dead Poets Society, where he has a group of college prep students gathered around him and says, "The powerful play goes on and you may contribute a verse." The powerful play goes on and you may contribute a verse." "What will your verse be?"

Obviously, the play is a metaphor for life and each of us in society's larger picture will have the opportunity to make some kind of contribution while we are here. The question for each of us in the grander scope of things is what will that contribution be?

This is precisely the same message that Mr. Alston delivers to the masses of people he encounters around the world. It is the same message that I am making an effort to convey to you through the writing of this book. As your financial situation vastly improves by applying the time honored principles you find written in these pages, you will be afforded numerous opportunities to use your wealth and new found economic wherewithal to help not only yourself, your family and loved ones but numerous individuals you may never even meet. Will you be a good steward over your finances? This will turn out to be an amazing test to see whether or not you are able to sustain your new found wealth by virtue of your generosity.

I have no doubt that if you follow the principles in this book that you will experience unparalleled economic success above and beyond anything you could ever hope to dream or imagine.

Through his program, Mr. Alston urges you to tap into the very core of your human existence and release the passion that resides there and ultimately drives you toward your goal. If you haven't found it yet, just keep living and keep following your dreams until you get to the point where you've chased them down and all of a sudden realize just exactly what it is that you desire to do with the remaining years of your life.

And when you do, think long and hard on the words Mr. Alston uses to close out his phenomenal program. Etch these words into your heart and strive to do your absolute best to achieve not only your economic goals but any goal you have in life. These are the words to the powerful poem that Mr. Alston uses to close out his program.

Be The Best

If you can't be a pine on top of the hill,
    Be a scrub in the valley but be;
The best little scrub by the side of the rill,
    Be a bush if you can't be a tree.

If you can't be a bush, be a bit of the grass,
    Some highway happier make;
If you can't be a muskie, then just be a bass,
    But the liveliest bass in the lake.

We can't all be captains, we've got to be crew,
    There's something for all of us here;
There's big work to do and there's lesser to do,
    But the task we must do is the near.

If you can't be a highway, then just be a trail,
    If you can['t be the sun, be a star;
It isn't by size that you win or you fail,
    Be the best of whatever you are.

Douglas Mallock

All That Glitters Is Not Gold

"For the goal is not the gold. Life is more
    than that after all;
The simple truth of the matter is just to rise
    each time that you fall."
Dr. Robert L. Lawson

Let me give you something to think about if you spend a lot of time being envious about many of your professional sports heroes. First, please note that I have tremendous respect and admiration for those athletes and entertainers in our society who have become rich and famous by using their God-given talents in such an adroit fashion.

I am not at all envious of what they have achieved and perhaps others would be less envious if they took enough time to do a little research and secure the facts for themselves. Perhaps if others just thought about it for a moment, maybe they would realize that only a select few in our society achieve the kind of financial stability that enables them to live and maintain a life of luxury for an indefinite period of time.

For every Kobe Bryant, Larry Bird, Brett Favre, Lebron James or Peyton Manning, the majority of their professional colleagues do not fare nearly as well. What you see on television over and over and over again are those who are constantly in the limelight. You are seeing the exceptions to the rule.

Here is the cold hard truth which gives so much validity and credence to the book you are currently holding in your hands. This next part that you read is the part that no one wants to talk about. It's the jaw dropping truth. Are you ready for it? All right, then, here it is.

Given that the average gridiron player's career in the NFL is three years, the average Green Bay salary of $440,000 means that after taxes, they earn less than $1,000,000 in total career earnings. This is further hampered by the fact there is no where else to play as leagues fold.

Here's another startling stat to think about. Within two years of retirement, 78% of NFL players are bankrupt or in severe financial distress.

The few who are able to rise above the masses are those who have mastered something far greater than their ability to earn money. They have mastered the art of learning how to keep it. Therein lies the true key to economic prosperity and massive financial success.

When you compare those who are rich and famous in our society to the millions upon millions of individuals who are not, there is a tremendous disparity between the two groups. How is it possible for those individuals who earn quite a bit over a short period of time to end up in such dire straits? Here's at least a part of the answer. (1). Greed. The greed of many who surround these amazingly talented and gifted athletes and provide them either with bad advice or take total advantage of their ineptness or lack of experience and (2) the false sense of security which surround those who become instant millionaires.

Here's the point. If one has never had a ton of money one minute and is suddenly elevated to "millionaire status" over night, the height can be dizzying. You can liken the experience to state lottery winners who suddenly discover "instant wealth" from the lucky draw of a state lottery ticket. The reality is that 70% of lottery winners will squander away their earnings in a few years.

The state of temporary insanity or euphoria that this rarified air and all of the money causes impedes one's ability to think clearly, reason logically and breathe freely. You've never been in this position before and to expect someone to think clearly about all of it is just unreasonable. I have actually had a former student of mine who won the Ohio lottery that was worth several million dollars at the time. True to form in relationship to what the majority of financial planners say, this individual ran through with every single penny in just a few short years.

The fact of the matter is this. If you have a good paying job and you have mastered the art of saving and investing money wisely and are handling your debt effectively without incurring additional debt, your chances of eventually acquiring and maintaining a wonderful lifestyle are far greater than the average professional athlete or average entertainer. Please note that I said average for as you know, there are exceptions to every rule.

Now, let's examine more closely why these athletes have a greater propensity to fail. Well, use some common sense and logic. Think about it.

(1). Living above their means. This is the number one issue that tends to be so problematic for these young people. Folks who've never had money have this innate largess or desire to impress other people, friends, parents, acquaintances etc. They develop that "I'm the woman. I'm the man" syndrome. Haven't you ever noticed the hordes of people who surround those who are on the verge of getting the "money?" If you've never had an opportunity to observe it, watch the NFL draft sometime. There are hordes of what I can "Hanger-oners."

Now, don't get me wrong. Obviously, there are those individuals who deserve to share in the reward of these young, talented and gifted people; however, don't you think there should be a limit?

Think for just a moment though. There is no logical way to reason with someone who has just hit the state lottery or signed a multimillion dollar contract to play a professional sport.

Who am I or you to tell these people how they should spend their money? How dare us! We are nobody. They are not going to listen to our advice not even when the golden financial parachute comes tumbling to the ground and surely it will, I am as sure of that as the air you are breathing at this precise moment. When their self inflated ego is devoid of air, then perhaps you will get their attention but if they remain full of haughty and arrogant pride, perhaps not. No one wants to admit failure when it comes to the mismanagement of economic resources.

Unfortunately, unless they are willing to do as you are doing, which is to build solid, financial success one step at a time, they will never regain their lofty, economic position. You may think these words are a bit harsh; however, the more enamored we are with ourselves, the more vulnerable we are to falling into those human-made traps that are designed to keep us impoverished.

What is another fallacy?

(2). Thinking their income is going to last forever. Think again! This false sense of security comes when one is lulled into thinking that their salary is self perpetuating. Unless a substantial portion of their earnings is wisely invested, that too shall end. With no education or experience in another field, where are they going to work? Planning for the future is undoubtedly a wise thing to do and many of these individuals are at a crossroads in their lives that they had never previously anticipated.

(3). They have no savings. If it's not a habit you've developed prior to becoming a millionaire, what makes you think that when you become one that you will automatically develop that habit? That is not the way life works. Whatever you did before you had the money is exactly what you will do once you've started making the big bucks. That spells a ton of trouble for those individuals who happen to be spendthrifts, love to shop, drive four or five cars and own four or five homes if not more. Status becomes the hot ticket. You are in it for show. Your desire is to impress, to flaunt and to be extravagant. It's hard to realize at this point that there's really no one you have or need to impress.

(4). No Investment plan. It would logically follow that if one has developed the habit to save that one would reach the point where one is able to invest. One precedes the other, however, one does not work unless the other has been in place for a substantial period of time.

(5). Unless dollars are properly invested, taxes will eat up a huge chunk of a professional athlete's revenue.

(6). What happens in the event that athlete is no longer able to perform at a high level? The unexpected happens. That financial cushion is no longer there to be a support.

The horror stories about professional athletes and movie stars who've had illustrious careers or their "moments in the sun" are abundant. We read about them extensively and we observe the lifestyles of the rich and famous in an endless manner. We are transfixed by their stories and we monitor their every move because of their charisma and their compelling, spellbinding ways and yet, many of them wind up on the streets like average citizens, away from the limelight and the glitter, once their money is gone, so are many of their so called friends who could more aptly be referred to as leeches.

I encourage you to see if you can learn the lesson that I am trying to learn from all of this. Take stock of your own abilities, talents and skills. Don't let what you see happening to many others on the road of life happen to you. Learn, if you can, vicariously from the mistakes of others and do a much better job of preparing for and planning your own future by putting what you learn from this book into action in your own life. Your ability to act on the principles in this book is what will empower you to help not only yourself but millions of other people who may be traveling down a similar road themselves.

Student Testimonials

"When the student is ready, the teacher will appear."

Buddhist Proverb

Whether or not this book ever makes it to the New York Times Best Sellers List is not relevant. The thing that validated the content of what I was teaching was the responses I kept getting from my students. After a while, I realized that I needed to get this material into a book so that I could reach the masses of people who had a need for it.

When I wrote in an earlier chapter that I was motivated by my students and the impact that the material was having on their lives, I was not kidding. This, in my humble opinion, is what makes a book a best seller and for that reason only, it already is.

I want you to read these wonderful comments from Rachel Higgins and as you do I want you to give some serious thought as to how you can begin to apply the financial ideas I've reviewed in this book to your own life. That's really all I want you to do. How can you put the ideas in this book to constructive use in your own life?

Here are Rachel's exact words. "This is the third class I've taken from you and your classes just keep getting better and better!

I shared with you a little bit before class how your classes have helped me. After your first class, I met with my boyfriend for lunch and I shared with him some of your ideas on how to save money. Since then we've made a commitment to each other that we'd save a certain amount of money from each paycheck to start saving for a house. If we stay committed to this plan for two years we'll have almost $40,000.00 to put towards a house.

I'm 19 years old. If I hadn't taken your class, I would never have thought about saving for a house or saving at all. You're the only person who's ever stressed (to me) the importance of starting to save at a young age.

In today's class, I really enjoyed hearing you encourage everyone in our class to be leaders. I know I keep mentioning the mindset of people in Southern, Ohio but I can't help but to talk about how important your classes are for the people in this area.

I believe that everyone is a leader and many people have no idea how much they influence those around them and I honestly believe you are helping people to see the leader they have within.

I recently started helping with the teens at my dad's church. When they first asked me to start helping, all I could think about was all of my faults and how imperfect I really am but then, I started to think about some of the things I learned in class about myself and the things I have to offer that are good and positive so I agreed to lead praise and worship service for the teens as well as preaching when needed.

I can't say this enough, if I hadn't taken your classes, I highly doubt I would have agreed to help with the teens at church and I know for a fact that I would never have started saving. Thank you for taking the time to come and talk.

God Bless You!

P.S. I know I'm supposed to pick out the "best" part of the session for me but, I can't because you said you only want 1 and 1/2 to 2 pages and since everything was _amazing_, I don't have enough paper! ☺

Author's comments:

Can you imagine how my confidence level was boosted by these positive words I received from Rachel? When I wrote to Rachel and followed up with an email to see if I could use her comments in this book, she responded on June 13, 2010 with this brief note. I am including these additional comments from Rachel so that readers have a good idea about how serious this young woman is.

Hello Dr. Lawson,

I'm sorry it's taken me so long to respond. I just finished all my finals. I'm sure you know how crazy finals week can be ☺
Thank you for the letter you sent! I sat down today and decided to check to see if maybe you had emailed me as well. Of course you can use what I've said in your book.

There was no need to ask. I loved all of your classes. Just to update you, my boyfriend and I have saved almost $3,000.00 in less than two months. (Not bad for 2 fulltime college students.)
I've taken some of the things you taught me in class and applied them to my life. My boyfriend has as well. Thank you for the motivation! I've already talked to a few of my friends about your Dare to Be a Millionaire Course and told them how

much they would benefit by attending. I wish you the best of luck and I promise to work to get to that class.

Rachel

Author's Response:

Earlier in this book, you read where Megan Weidig was planning to set $50.00 aside from each of her paychecks. Here, you can see where Rachel has joined forces with her significant partner to save a considerable amount more. Here's the point. We can all make significant progress where money is concerned. Each of us needs to do something that is comfortable for us and our style of living. More so than anything else, the real key as these folks have demonstrated is to do something.

If Rachel and her partner are able to keep this momentum going for the next 15 to 20 years, they will be well on their way to achieving millionaire status. This savings opportunity they have started will begin to grow exponentially as they invest their dollars wisely by virtue of good economic counseling. What they have started will take on a life of its own and what they do will not only be beneficial to themselves but to many others.

Rachel is a very mature young woman and she is already making a significant impact on the youth around her by the example that she sets. I can just imagine over time how much stronger and more powerful her influence is going to become. That is exactly what this process that we are discussing is all about.

Instead of acquiring endorsements and comments from notable celebrities, high profile authors and recognizable entertainers to grace the cover of my book, I wanted to use a more practical approach by providing opportunities for people like you who are in the trenches every single day. Joyce Weichelman, for example, is an excellent teacher who has attended a number of my seminars. Her comments appear on the back of my book. Joyce understands very clearly what individuals must do to attract wealth into their lives. Take a few moments to read her comments as well as the comments of some of my other professional colleagues. They are right on target.

Another very talented and gifted seminar participant by the name of Tammy Davis had this to say. "I would be very interested in taking the Dare to Be A Millionaire seminar. I honestly don't need to have a million dollars but, I want my family to be comfortable. We don't need a mansion or a country club membership or "status." We are who we are. I want to learn different methods of saving money. I do not want to learn about "banking level" statistics – but rather, the simple things that make a big difference.

I read an article about paying an extra $36.00 a month on the interest of a payment—I believe it was a house payment that literally thousands of dollars in interest could be saved.

This is probably low level information but for me, the low level information mixed with your extremely motivating tactics would be an uplifting experience. When I left your class last week, I had an overwhelming desire to go straight home, exercise, clean house, teach my four year old to read, etc. You definitely have the power to motivate and that motivation combined with financial ideas and instruction would be excellent."

Students like Joyce, Rachel and Tammy are the ones who keep me focused on my work and empower me to keep right on doing what it is that I do. There's a part of me that feels like this book is quite different from any other book on the market that deals specifically with financial issues and how to obtain wealth. The reason why I feel that it is different is because of exactly what Tammy said.

Her observation is quite relevant. This book not only provides readers with information that will enable them to increase their wealth; It also provides them with the empowerment tools that are necessary for them to feel motivated as they do so. This added bonus is the kind of thing that will provide readers with a wonderful opportunity to be exposed to ideas that will not only enhance their financial positions in life but will permeate the very fabric of their lives in other areas as well.

Nuggets of Wisdom: On the Road to Greatness

When you have a talent, a gift or a skill,
To be shared with someone you know;
Transfer the knowledge from your heart to theirs,
And enable their spirit to grow.

Our purpose in life is to help others see,
Their vast potential within;
For if they can cultivate some unique skill,
It heightens their passion to win.

You've traversed so many lessons in life,
And truly have so much to give;
Show how to sidestep the potholes of strife,
And teach others how they can live.

The nuggets of wisdom that you have acquired,
Are not to be hidden from view;
They are to be polished and put on display,
So that others will see what to do.

Courage, conviction, compassion and hope,
Are but a few of the jewels;
Goals, purpose, action and scope,
Add to your storehouse of tools.

As you press on in your quest to achieve,
The vision held deep in your heart;
You will receive what you truly believe,
As you follow the course that you chart.

The labor you exert will bring into being,
The things you so ardently seek;
As long as you learn to apply what you know,
Week after bonafide week.

The time to take charge of your life is right now,
As you work out a diligent plan;
You can show others how to be great,
But you just have to know that you can.

© 2010 Dr. Robert L. Lawson

My philosophy of life has been shaped, molded and influenced by what I would consider to be some of the most powerful minds in existence. That would include my aunt Nora Faye Lawson who introduced me to life game changers like Henry David Thoreau, Ralph Waldo Emerson, Rudyard Kipling and the like.

Later on in life, when I needed them most, I would discover on my own such notable influences and Dr. Norman Vincent Peale and Dr. Robert Schuller. These were powerful minds that understood the tremendous power that resides in a person's attitude toward life and how to capitalize on the power of positive thinking and doing.

I would go on to be further influenced by Dr. Claude M. Bristol, Dr. David Schwartz, Dr. John Maxwell, Dr. Wayne Dyer and others too numerous to mention here. Powerful poets and their writings have had a significant influence as well. Those would include such personalities as Walt Whitman, Edgar Alan Gest, Edgar Alan Poe and many, many, many others.

Then, after all of that even, when my grandmother passed in 1982 and I happened to go to the old home place just to see what was left after family members had taken everything of value, my foot just happened to kick an old book that was lying on the living room floor. It was all that remained. Ironically enough, it turned out to be one of the greatest treasures that one could find imaginable. The editor of the book was a man named James Tilley. The title of the book was Masters of the Situation: Some Secrets of Success and Power. That book contained some of the most powerful writings I had ever encountered. It was replete with information on determination, manners, reserve, possibilities, country boys, city boys, the human will and so much more. It contained 767 pages of some of the most dynamic material I had ever read on the development of human potential. It was a book that would change my life forever because I knew the value of these principles and I knew that if I could take the time to devour as much of this material as possible and develop a conceptual framework into which I could utilize it effectively that I would be able to help a significant number of individuals with what I had discovered and that is exactly what I am doing through the seminars, conferences, workshops and courses that I conduct today.

Our approach to life is an individual approach. We are all different and yet in many ways we are similar. One of Lord Byron's quotes in the book I speak about says this.

"From my youth upward, my spirit walked not with the souls of men nor looked upon the earth with human eyes. The aim of their existence was not mine. The thirst of their ambition was not mine. My joys, my, strengths, my passions and my powers made me a stranger."

That is a most insightful and enlightening passage. It makes us take a good look at who we are or who we think we are. What are your joys, your strengths, your purpose and your passion? Once we get to the point where we can answer those questions individually and for ourselves is at that precise moment when we will begin the journey of making our greatest contributions. It is a most notable thing to contemplate.

Numerous principles have been guiding forces in my life which are not limited to but include my faith and my belief in God. I consider these beliefs to be the true foundation of my success. The seven key principles that all of my students are pretty much aware of, I have shared since I can remember. They are also staples in my foundation. They are motivation, action, commitment, change, enthusiasm, attitude and determination. The Bible serves as my base.

These concepts are such a part of my life's philosophy that I can lecture for hours upon hours about the content of each principle. They are literally an extension of who I am. They are the principles that generate the power that is essential to achieving wealth and the development of an abundance mentality. They serve as the catalyst behind all great achievement.

I did not want to finish this book without at least mentioning these incredible attributes. I must tell you that out of the 100's of quotes with which I am familiar that there are several that if we fully understood and applied their content, we could possibly turn the world on its edge. Certainly, I want to take some time to share a few of them with you before we get into the section on the shorter aphorisms and bring this book to a close. I also want to take a few moments to explain why each quote is so powerful and if taken seriously could be a major catalyst to inspire others to act.

Here's a powerful passage to think seriously about.

"If you advance confidently in the direction of your dreams and endeavor to live the life which you have imagined, you will meet with a success unexpected in common hours. You will put some things behind, will pass an invisible boundary, new, universal and more liberal laws will establish themselves around and within you and you will live with the license of a higher order of beings."

Henry David Thoreau

I've always said that competence begets confidence. The more we know about a particular thing, the more our confidence grows. Then it becomes as Thoreau has said, each step we take forward puts us closer to the goals we have set for ourselves. And what's really amazing is that other doors begin to open for you that you didn't even recognize or know that were there. It is a powerful concept; continue to put it into operation.

Here's a powerful quote by Dr. Myles Monroe. See what you think of this.

"Vision is the juice of life. It is the prerequisite for passion and the source of persistence. When you have vision, you know how to stay in the race and complete it. Now, proverbs 18:16 shows how you will accomplish your vision. A man's gift makes room for him. You were designed to be known for your gift. It is the gift that will enable you to fulfill your dream."

Dr. Myles Monroe

Wow! Seeing yourself successful in a particular endeavor is the thing that enables you to keep on keeping on. It's what keeps you fired up. The innate talent, gift or ability that you have is what you are supposed to be using for the benefit of others. What is it and why have you not taken the time to fully cultivate it yet?

Here are some nuggets of wisdom from the Greek philosopher, Heraclitus.

"The soul is dyed the color of its thoughts. Think only on those things that are in line with your principles and can bear the full light of day. The content of your character is your choice. Day by day, what you choose, what you think and what you do is who you become. Your integrity is your destiny. It is the light that guides your way."

What you spend your time thinking about is exactly what helps to mold and shape your character and helps to determine the person you will become. Whatever you decide to focus on is what you will get more of.

Here are some wise words from Patanjali.

"When you are inspired by some great purpose, some extraordinary project, all your thoughts break their bonds, your mind transcends limitations, your consciousness expands in every direction and you find yourself in a new great and wonderful world. Dormant forces, faculties and talents become alive and you discover yourself to be a greater person by far than you ever dreamed yourself to be."

As you move forward in life to discover your ultimate purpose for being here, this will add tremendous fuel to the fire that drives you from within to realize some of your key objectives in life. Not everything has to be life shattering. The small contributions that people make are just as important as the big ones and sometimes even more so.

It's sometimes amazing though because once you've completed one particular objective, you can many times see your way clear to complete the next one. Your confidence grows with each completion and when you do take a look back, sometimes it's amazing to see just how far you've come.

Cushman K. Davis had this to say:

"Those who have achieved success are those who have worked, read, thought more than was absolutely necessary; who have not been content with knowledge sufficient for the present need but have sought additional knowledge and stored it away for emergency reserve. It is the superfluous labor that equips one for everything that counts most in life."

These too are some extremely powerful words. Firstly, it is incumbent upon each one of us to define what success actually means for each of us. None of us should be held captive by someone else's definition but neither should we use that as an excuse to settle for less than what we want out of life. I'm going to share with you one last, long quote that correlates strongly with this one because the same message is inherent in both. The one key word that links them together inextricably is "labor."

Sir Joshua Reynolds, the 17th Century artist had this to say:

"You must have no dependence on your own genius. If you have great talents, industry will improve them. If you have but moderate abilities, industry will supply their deficiency. Nothing is denied to well directed labor. Nothing is to be obtained without it. Not to enter into metaphysical discussions on the nature or essence of genius, I will assert that assiduity unabated by difficulty and a disposition eagerly directed to the object of its pursuit will produce effects similar to those which some call the result of natural powers."

I know that what I am about to say will be questioned and I hope that it will but not without some serious analytical thought. It is my belief that anyone who completely understands this passage has the ability to achieve unlimited success.

However you wish to use these terms interchangeably, work, labor or industry, they all mean the same thing. With a comprehensive and diligent work ethic, you can acquire almost anything you want.

How much time, how much energy and how much effort are you willing to expend to bring about the change you desire? That is the real question.

These ideas are truly difference makers. This book was designed to keep you focused on the goals you have set for yourself. The information here is powerful beyond measure. If you can just do some of the things that are inherent in these pages, you will soon find yourself even further along the road you are traveling than you are now and closing in fast on the desires of your heart. Enjoy the quotes that follow to keep you inspired,

make you think and inform and enrich your
experience even more.

**If you would be wealthy, think
of saving as well as getting.**

Ben Franklin

**Money was never a big motivation
for me except as a way to keep score.
The real excitement is playing the
game.**

Donald Trump

**Ordinary riches can be stolen; real
riches cannot. In your soul are
infinitely precious things that
cannot be taken from you.**

Oscar Wilde

**The real measure of your wealth
is how much you'd be worth if
you lost all your money.**

**Whatsoever thy hand findeth to do,
do it with thy might for there is no**

work, nor device nor wisdom in the grave whither thou goest.

Ecclesiastes 9:10.

Money and success don't change people;
They merely amplify what is already there.

Will Smith

Happiness is not the mere possession of money; it lies in the joy of achievement, in the thrill of creative effort.

Franklin D. Roosevelt

Your own resolution to succeed is the most important factor in success.

Abraham Lincoln

Look to your health; and if you have it, praise God, and value it next to a good conscience; for health is the second blessing that we mortals are capable of, a blessing that money cannot buy.

Izaac Walton

The very first step to building wealth is to spend less than you make.

Brian Koslow

If money is your hope for independence, you will never have it. The only real security that a man will have in this world is a reserve of knowledge, experience and ability.

Henry Ford

The little money I have, that is wealth, but the things I have for which I would not take money, that is my treasure.

Robert Brault

**The best way for a person to have happy
thoughts is to count his blessings and
not his cash.**

Anonymous

**Empty pockets never held anyone back;
Only empty heads and empty hearts
can do that.**

Norman Vincent Peale

**The way to wealth is as plain as the
way to market. It depends chiefly on
two words, industry and frugality, that
is waste neither time nor money, but
make the best of both. Without
industry and frugality, nothing will do.
With them, everything.**

Benjamin Franklin

**I have a problem with too much money.
I can't invest it fast enough, and because
I reinvest it, more money comes in.
Yes, the rich do get richer.**

Robert Kiyosaki

Robert Kiyosaki has a problem with too much money. What a wonderful problem to have because it gives you unlimited options.

Dr. Robert L. Lawson

**You can only become truly accomplished at something you love. Don't make money
your goal. Instead, pursue the things you
love doing and then do them so well that people can't take their eyes off of you.**

Maya Angelou

Formal education will make you a living; Self education will make you a fortune.

You have not lived a perfect day even though you have earned your money, unless you have done something for someone who can never repay you.

The art is not in making money but in keeping it.

Money is usually attracted, not pursued.

Jim Rohn

You cannot motivate the best people
with money. Money is just a way to
keep score.
The best people in any field are
motivated by passion.

Eric S. Raymond

Success does not lie in what we have
achieved but in the opposition we have
overcome to reach our goals.

Marian Wright Edelmann

There is only one way to achieve
something and that is to pursue it with
everything you've got.

Scot Hamilton

First, have a definite, clear practical
ideal—a goal, an objective. Second,
have the necessary means to achieve
your ends – wisdom, money, materials
and methods. Third, adjust all your
means to that end.

Aristotle

Success is almost totally dependent upon drive and persistence. The extra energy required to make another effort or try another approach is the secret of winning.

Vince Lombardi Jr.

Effort only fully releases its reward after a person refuses to quit.

Napoleon Hill

Success is knowing your purpose in life, growing to your maximum potential and sowing seeds that benefit others.

Dr. John Maxwell

You will become as small as your controlling desire or as great as your dominant aspiration.

James Allen

You are where you are and what you are because of what you believe yourself to be. Change your beliefs and you change your reality.

Brian Tracy

Optimism is the one quality more associated with success and happiness than any other.

Everything that is truly great and inspiring is created by the individual who can labor in freedom.

Albert Einstein

Therefore, I say unto you what things soever you desire, when ye pray, believe that ye receive them and ye shall have them.

Mark 11:24

In all thy ways acknowledge Him and He shall direct thy paths.

Proverbs 3:6

**Commit to the Lord whatever you do.
And your plans will succeed.**

Proverbs 16:3

**Many are the plans of a man's heart but
it is the Lord's purposes that prevail.**

Proverbs 19:21

**For I know the plans I have for you.
Plans to prosper you and not harm you.
Plans to give you hope and a future.**

Jeremiah 29:11

Occupations of Self-Made Millionaires

These entries are a partial listing taken directly from *The Millionaire Next Door*, written by Dr. Thomas J. Stanley and Dr. William Danko adapted by Dr. Robert L. Lawson

Accountants

Moving and Storage

Auctioneers

Newspaper Publisher

Advertising Executives

Nursing Home

Attorneys

Office Supplies

Authors

Orthopedic Surgeon

Beauty Salon Owner- Managers

Owner/College President

Clergyman – Lecturer

Paint Removal/Medal

Cleaning

Civil Engineers
Personal Injury Lawyer

Dairy Farmers

Pest Control Services

Department Store Owners

Pharmaceuticals

Direct Mail Services

President/Owner Mutual Funds

Mutual Funds

Fast Food Restaurants
Property Owner/Developer

Human Resource Consulting Services

Real Estate

Independent Investment Managers

Restaurant Owner

Insurance Agent

Sand and Gravel

Janitorial Contractors

Service Station Store/

Chain Owner

Lecturer

Travel Agency Owner

Liquor Wholesaler

Vegetables Farmer

Market Sales professional

Welding Contractor

Wholesale Grocery

116

101 Things You Can Do to Earn Money

"Life rewards action."

Dr. Phil

If you've read through the book and you've gotten this far, first let me say, congratulations! You are obviously pretty serious about generating some additional revenue. Some of the ideas you see here may appeal to you. Many of them probably won't. Their real purpose though is to get you to start thinking creatively and innovatively about some of the things you might wish to explore or do. This is just a start.

Some of the best ideas start out in the mind, get transferred to paper and the rest is history. Whether it's getting a job or starting a business, it only takes one good idea and you'll soon have additional dollars flowing into your pocket.

Just ask the guys who came up with the slogan, "Life is good." They put it on T-shirts and sold them and after awhile, the idea caught on, they started small by selling the T-shirts locally and now they have an operation that literally generates millions of dollars as a result of their persistence in following through on this little idea that turned out to generate massive success.

Millions of people have great ideas. They just don't do anything with them. That could be the difference between you and them. When I was little, we used to play with squirt guns or water pistols.

Years later, a gentleman would invent the Super Soaker, a huge squirt gun that had instant market appeal and turned him into a millionaire once it got to the marketplace. What if you or I had thought of that and were persistent enough to get it to the market place? Hmmmmm.

What about the two guys who came up with the concept for the game called Trivial Pursuit and became millionaires when they sold the rights to a large game company? The ideas are endless and the best ones haven't even been invented yet. Maybe you will make the next great discovery.

At any rate, these 101 ideas can be used as a platform to stir your creativity and imagination even more as you think about some of the things you like to do. After all, your imagination is the greatest nation on earth. I'm going to close this book with an awesome statement I heard Doc Rivers say on television the other night when I was watching the Los Angeles Lakers play the Boston Celtics during the fifth game of the NBA championship. The statement was so awesome that I had to get up and write it down. The head coach of the Boston Celtics said, "We already know the answers to the test, we just have to go out there and execute." Well, there it is folks. That's pretty much the answer to at least how some of life works. That's sort of the way it always is. We know what to do, we just don't do what we know. Now, that you have read this book in its entirety and you know a plethora of the concepts, ideas and principles that it takes to become successful, what are you going to do about it? That's the real question. You see, it's like Doc said. You have some answers now. The question is, Are you going to execute? I encourage you to Dare to Be a Millionaire. The Celtics eventually lost to the Lakers. It doesn't mean, these principles don't work; It means that on that particular night, the

Lakers were a better team. They executed their game plan more effectively. Will you?

1. Go back to school and expand your education.
2. If your job has ended, start looking for another one.
3. Scan the newspapers to see if anything fits your skill sets.
4. Get a part-time job to augment your income.
5. Start your own business.
6. Start an Internet business
7. Form a team, develop a brain trust and work with others on your idea.
8. Do in house child care.
9. Conduct a seminar
10. Conduct a workshop
11. Knit/Crochet
12. Become a university adjunct
13. Do library research
14. Tutor
15. Write letters, resumes and type papers for others
16. Sell Avon
17. Sell Amway
18. Sell Mary Kay Products
19. Join the army or some other branch of the armed services
20. Contact an internet business advertised on T.V.
21. Learn to build computers
22. Become an information referral service for others.
23. Work in a restaurant.
24. Deliver newspapers.
25. Start a chauffeur or limousine service.
26. Create a product
27. Write a book
28. Make a CD

29. **Make a DVD**
30. **Place information on a Jump Drive or MP3 player**
31. **Get on American Idol**
32. **Find someone in your community who needs help.**
33. **Start a grocery delivery service.**
34. **Volunteer your services (It's a way to get known).**
35. **Create a one man/one woman show**
36. **Sell produce on the roadside**
37. **Tailor clothing**
38. **Write a movie script**
39. **Write a novel**
40. **Put on a program at your local library**
41. **Take care of someone's pets**
42. **Run errands**
43. **Start a service to assist the elderly**
44. **Apply for and get a grant**
45. **Give blood**
46. **Have a yard/garage sale**
47. **Do calligraphy**
48. **Do in home health care**
49. **Sell real estate**
50. **Sell insurance**
51. **Run for public office**
52. **Become a radio announcer**
53. **Write/publish news articles**
54. **Subscribe to the Wall Street Journal**
55. **Grocery shop for others**
56. **Set up a lawn care/grass cutting service**
57. **Paint someone's house**
58. **Strip and tie tobacco**
59. **Work for a local farmer**
60. **Coach a sport**
61. **Play guitar in a club**
62. **Teach someone a skill**
63. **Play piano**
64. **Recite Poetry**

65. Do an E book
66. Work with building contractors
67. Check in with the pipefitters' union
68. Check in with the carpenters' union
69. Apply to a truck driving school
70. Get your high school equivalency diploma
71. Get an associate degree
72. Get a baccalaureate degree
73. Get a master's degree
74. Get a doctorate
75. Enroll in community college courses
76. Become a machine transcriptionist
77. Become a billings rep
78. Become a receptionist
79. Become a barber
80. Become a restaurant owner
81. Become a custodian
82. Set up an advertising firm
83. Secure a state contract for services
84. Promote a diet that works.
85. Promote a fitness/exercise program that works
86. Become highly knowledgeable in a field and work it.
87. Write a play
88. Invest in yourself through money, education and books
89. Ask, Seek and Knock, Matthew 7:7
90. Take a lesser paying job to get back to where you were
91. Build your relationship with God
92. Build solid relationships with other people
93. Satisfy your relicensure requirements
94. Satisfy your recertification requirements
95. Build your reputation with others and establish credibility
96. In all thy ways acknowledge Him and He will direct thy paths

97. **Put a performance together and display it on Youtube**
98. **Become a census taker**
99. **Set up a moving company**
100. **Contact an investment company that can help you grow $$**
101. **Take a public speaking course**

About the Author

Dr. Robert L. Lawson has amassed over 36 years of cumulative experience serving as a teacher, administrator, adjunct professor, business entrepreneur, consultant and writer.

Currently, he teaches English, poetry, leadership and three introductory college level courses on composition, research and specific applications of research as it applies to literature.

Dr. Lawson teaches at Georgetown Jr.-Sr. High School and at the Ohio University branches in Chillicothe and Zanesville, Ohio.

He holds a bachelor's degree with a major in English from the University of Rio Grande, a Master's Degree from Marshall University with a concentration in 17th century literature in the field of English and a doctorate from Nova Southeastern University in Educational Administration.

Dr. Lawson has developed and taught numerous curriculums in the field of Human Potential, Growth and Development which includes such topics as How to Stay Motivated to Win, Maximizing Your Potential for Greatness, Change Your Thinking; Change Your Life, Diversity: An Approach That Works, Sexual Harassment, How to Make an Effective Presentation, On Becoming an Effective Leader, Leadership: Nuggets of Wisdom, Ordinary People Achieving Extraordinary Things, Oh Yes We Can! Black Achievement in America, Achieving Excellence in the Classroom and his most recent sensational seminar and book entitled, "Dare to Be A Millionaire."

In addition, he has authored Destined for Greatness, The Power of Optimism, Ageless Wisdom and, The Triumph of the Spirit.

He is an outstanding presenter and professional speaker who mixes inspiration with humor and wit while leaving audiences feeling spellbound and empowered in the process. Dr. Lawson currently resides in Portsmouth, Ohio with his lovely wife, Shannon, and two of his three wonderful sons.

When he is not teaching or lecturing, he is giving empowerment presentations around the globe. His email address is rlawson68@hotmail.com and his mailing address is P.O. Box 2052
Portsmouth, Ohio 45662